SOCIAL SKILLS FOR TWEENS

Boost Confidence, Tackle Social Anxiety, Charm People around You, Build Genuine Relationships, and Much More. A Practical Guide for Pre-Teens to Become Bright Teenagers

INSTANT RELIEF

© Copyright 2022 VOX PUBLISHING HOUSE - All rights reserved.

The content contained within this book may not be reproduced, duplicated, or transmitted without direct written permission from the author or the publisher.
Under no circumstances will any blame or legal responsibility be held against the publisher, or author, for any damages, reparation, or monetary loss due to the information contained within this book, either directly or indirectly.

Legal Notice:
This book is copyright protected. It is only for personal use. You cannot amend, distribute, sell, use, quote or paraphrase any part, or the content within this book, without the consent of the author or publisher.

Disclaimer Notice:
Please note the information contained within this document is for educational and entertainment purposes only. All effort has been executed to present accurate, up to date, reliable, complete information. No warranties of any kind are declared or implied. Readers acknowledge that the author is not engaging in the rendering of legal, financial, medical, or professional advice. The content within this book has been derived from various sources. Please consult a licensed professional before attempting any techniques outlined in this book.
By reading this document, the reader agrees that under no circumstances is the author responsible for any losses, direct or indirect, that are incurred as a result of the use of information contained within this document, including, but not limited to, errors, omissions, or inaccuracies.

https://www.facebook.com/voxpublishinghouse

Don't miss our gift for you!

Go to the page
https://voxpublishinghouse.aweb.page/social-skills-for-tweens

or scan the QR code

Table of Contents

Introduction 7

CHAPTER 1 - What Are Social Skills? 9
    The Importance of Having Social Skills 10
    Necessary Characteristics to Develop Social Skills 11
    Types of Social Skills 13
    The Benefits of Having Good Social Skills 16
    Lack of Social Skills 16
    Quiz 17

CHAPTER 2 - Who Are Tweens? 19
    Tweens 20
    Challenges Tweens Face 20
    Changes During Tweens Years 21
    Questionnaire: Get to Know Yourself Better! 26

CHAPTER 3 - What Is Social Anxiety? 33
    What Is Social Anxiety Disorder? 33
    Social Anxiety vs. Shyness 34
    Symptoms of Social Anxiety Disorder 35
    Causes of Social Anxiety 36
    Self-Assessment: Do I Struggle with Social Anxiety Disorder? 41

CHAPTER 4 - Boosting Self-Esteem and Confidence 45
    Self-Esteem Defined 45
    Causes of Low Self-Esteem in Pre-Teens 48
    Signs of Low Self-Esteem 49
    How to Improve Self-Esteem 52

CHAPTER 5 - Making Friends 55
    The Importance of Having Genuine Friendships 56
    How to Find Good Friends 57
    How to Handle Various Situations 62

CHAPTER 6 - The Road to Independence 65
    What Does It Mean to Be Independent? 65
    Are People Who Need Help Dependent? 66
    Independence 68
    The Importance of Independence 69
    How to Make Better Decisions 71

CHAPTER 7 - Using Technology 75
Why Too Much Screen Time Is Detrimental 76
Use of Social Media, Why or Why Not? 78
Smart Usage of Technology 80
Smart Social Networking 82

CHAPTER 8 - Managing Body Changes 85
So, What Happens? 85
Welcome to Puberty! 86
Changes in Boys During Puberty 88
Changes in Girls During Puberty 88
When Does Puberty Start and End? 89
5 Ways to Cope with Puberty and Your Changing Body 91

CHAPTER 9 - Channeling Your Emotions 95
Importance of Channeling Your Emotions 95
The Art of Mindfulness and Positive Thinking 96
Benefits of Channeling Your Emotions 97
Exercises to Channel Emotions Effectively 99
So, Where Does That Leave You? 102

Conclusion 105

References 107

Introduction

You probably look at any adult person and think, "wow, they've got it all together," or "I can't wait to be an adult." The truth or the secret that many grown-ups don't tell you is that everyone is struggling. Most people struggle with self-confidence and anxiety, which has become the norm for many people these days. You don't have to fret; every problem has a solution. This is why you always see people on the subway or waiting at the doctor's office, reading a self-help book. Books are powerful, and this book can help you develop the necessary social skills to prepare you for your teen years.

The book will first explain what social skills are and the characteristics you need to develop to be successful in these skills. You will also have a better understanding of this stage of your life and what it means to be a tween. Then we'll discuss certain issues that many tweens struggle with, like social anxiety and self-esteem. You will find tips on handling these issues so they won't have a big impact on your life.

You may have many friends, but have you ever wondered if these friendships are genuine? In this book, you will learn what it means to have genuine friendships and the traits to look for when making new friends.

The good news is that you are no longer a child, meaning you will have to start exploring life independently and take responsibility for your own decisions. This isn't as scary as it sounds; it is actually pretty cool and liberating. You will find tips on how to handle life's difficult situations and how to make decisions and understand that they always have consequences.

Technology is a big part of your life - you probably don't go anywhere without your cell phone, and you probably live on Instagram or TikTok. However, social media isn't always good for you; instead of letting it hurt you or avoiding it altogether, learn how to be smart about it. You will find tips on handling technology and using social media without letting it affect you, overwhelm you, or hurt your mental health.

Is your body starting to change? Don't worry; this is very normal at this stage of your life. The book will help you understand these changes and how to cope with them. They are a part of growing up, and everyone goes through it. The book will end by providing you with healthy ways to channel your emotions and tips on thinking positively and being happy.

Prepare yourself for an interesting journey that will help you understand yourself better and become the cool and collected person you have always wanted to be.

Chapter 1: What Are Social Skills?

You have probably heard the words "social skills" thrown around in various conversations. People always stress the importance of cultivating these skills and how useful they will be to help take you far in life. You probably think, "Great; I will improve my social skills to be a social butterfly and make more friends." Yes, having social skills can help you widen your friend circle. However, what exactly do people mean by social skills? Most people think you understand what they are already, so no one bothers explaining them to you. You shouldn't feel bad; many people of all ages don't fully understand the meaning behind social skills.

Social skills are tools you use to interact and communicate with others and help you develop healthy relationships. These skills can prevent misunderstandings between you and others since they allow you to communicate effectively and clearly. You will not only understand what people are saying, but you will also be able to guess what they aren't saying. Social skills can help you understand their gestures and read their body language.

For instance, you see that your friend isn't acting like themselves. They aren't crying or anything, but they aren't joking like they usually do or aren't paying attention in class. Here you will use your social skills to read your friend's body language and understand that something isn't right. Instead of asking them what's wrong when you are around other people, you wait until you both are alone. If they tell you what is upsetting them, the trick is to listen patiently without jumping in and telling them your opinion. However, if they tell you that they don't want to talk about it, don't push it and give just them some space. This will show them that you respect their needs, and they may even come to you when they are ready to talk.

By nature, people are sociable creatures, and as a result, they have different ways of communicating with one another that don't just depend on their words. They can communicate using tone of voice, body language, the volume of their voices, gestures, facial cues, and verbal language. So to develop your social skills, you should focus on how you talk and interact with others. Focus on what people are trying to communicate to you, even when they aren't using their words.

The Importance of Having Social Skills

There is no denying that social situations aren't easy. They aren't easy for grown-ups either; they just know more about hiding their discomfort. However, having social skills can make you feel at ease in these situations. In time, you will begin to feel more confident in yourself and show your sense of humor, and making new friends will get easier. The easier you handle these situations, the more confident you will feel in yourself. You are growing up, and you are no longer a child. A couple of years ago, you may have been able to get away with many things, but now you are at the age when you'll start to develop the necessary skills to help you get along with others. These abilities will also teach you to become more independent so you won't have to rely on your parents to help you make friends or speak up for you. Social skills will make it easier for you to make new friends, enjoy the ones you already have, create stronger bonds, and get along with your classmates. In a couple of years, you will become a teenager, so this is the perfect time to start watching people older than you to develop these skills for yourself.

Necessary Characteristics to Develop Social Skills

What is it like to have social skills? Well, first, there are certain personality traits that you need to start with and then build on to grow your own skills.

Listen Intently

Many people don't listen; they just wait for their turn to speak, and guess what? It shows, and the other person knows when you aren't really listening. When truly listening to someone, focus on what they are saying. It is more than just staying quiet; pay attention to everything they are trying to communicate to you, even the things they aren't saying out loud. This may sound challenging because you aren't a mind reader, but it is easier than you think, just remain focused and don't allow anything to distract you the same way you do when you watch the newest episode of your favorite TV show.

Remember in Stranger Things, how Will was trying to tell Mike that he needs him, but instead of talking about himself, he pretended he was talking about El instead? After his conversation, Will turned away and cried because he felt alone. Although Mike was listening to Will quietly, he still couldn't understand what his best friend was telling him and that he was crying next to him. Mike was too preoccupied was his relationship drama to pay attention to what Will wasn't saying. Luckily, Jonathan, Will's brother, really listened to his brother and understood that he was going through something. Listening is being there for the person instead of thinking of your own issues or what you will have for lunch.

As you learn to become a better listener, you will develop empathy which is part of what you need to interact with your friends. Empathy is identifying with another person's feelings and enabling you to put yourself in someone's shoes so that you can show them kindness and compassion. However, you can't do that without first listening and paying attention to what someone is saying. In your everyday life, strive to be a Jonathan, not a Mike.

Sharing Is Caring

You want to make friends, right? Sharing your stuff is one of the easiest ways to make people like you and make more friends. Share your snacks and things with your friends and classmates. This will help you make new friends and keep your current ones. When you share food with your friends, they will most likely share with you too, and when you share your stuff, you can enjoy them together instead of playing alone. Sharing is fun and will make you more popular.

Make Eye Contact

Making eye contact is necessary. Sometimes, looking at someone when you are talking to them can feel uncomfortable, so you often look away or at the ground, and you might not even know you're doing it. Being shy can also make it difficult to look someone in the eye when talking to you. Try to look at people when you are having a conversation with them - it makes the person think you have a lot of confidence and shows them that you are listening to them. You might find this a bit difficult at first, especially if you aren't used to it. This is normal. So take it slow, make eye contact for a couple of minutes, and look away for a few seconds when you feel uncomfortable, then make yourself look back up again, and so on. Keep doing this until eye contact begins to feel comfortable and normal to you. Eye contact is one of the most important social skills and will take you far in life.

Learn to Cooperate

You don't live alone in this world. In every area of your life, you will have to work with people - like on school projects, having a lab partner, or in a team playing a sport. When you find yourself in a group project, remember that you work together and not against each other. Learn how to cooperate and work with others as a team instead of working alone. Cooperation shows that you respect others and are willing to listen to their opinions rather than making all the decisions yourself. Not cooperating can also look like you are taking advantage of them and letting them do all the work, making you seem selfish. Remember, you are a part of a community, so it is necessary to be able to get along with everyone.

Manners Maketh the Man

If you watched Kingsman, then you have probably heard this saying before. Manners maketh the man or the woman. If there is one thing that all parents keep pointing out to their kids, it's how essential manners are. Having manners can help you make a great first impression and make you seem decent and likable. It is the simple things that show people that you are polite and respectful, like saying please and thank you, respecting your teachers and classmates, and treating people who serve you - like waiters - with decency. So next time your parents remind you to "have some manners," don't roll your eyes - actually listen to them. When you get older, you'll be surprised how much manners and treating people well will help you.

Types of Social Skills

Now that you understand what social skills can do for you let's look at the different types of social skills and how you can improve each.

Basic Social Skills

The first type is basic social skills. They are the foundation that you build on to get all the other skills. Learning these skills can help you communicate better with others. They include knowing how to start a conversation with someone, how to ask questions to keep the conversation fun and exciting, and how to end the conversation without seeming rude or disrespectful. These basic skills also include being a good listener, as mentioned above, without letting anything or anyone distracts you. You should also nod and smile when someone is talking to you to show them that you are engaged in the conversation. However, if someone is telling you a sad story, then react with the appropriate actions and expressions.

Improving this type of skill is so much fun and way more exciting than you think. Whether it's your friends, classmates, or siblings, try to initiate a conversation with them, ask them interesting questions, and show them that you care about what is going on in their lives without seeming nosy or pushy. The main thing is to listen to everything they tell you, even if you feel bored or have heard the story.

Advanced Social Skills

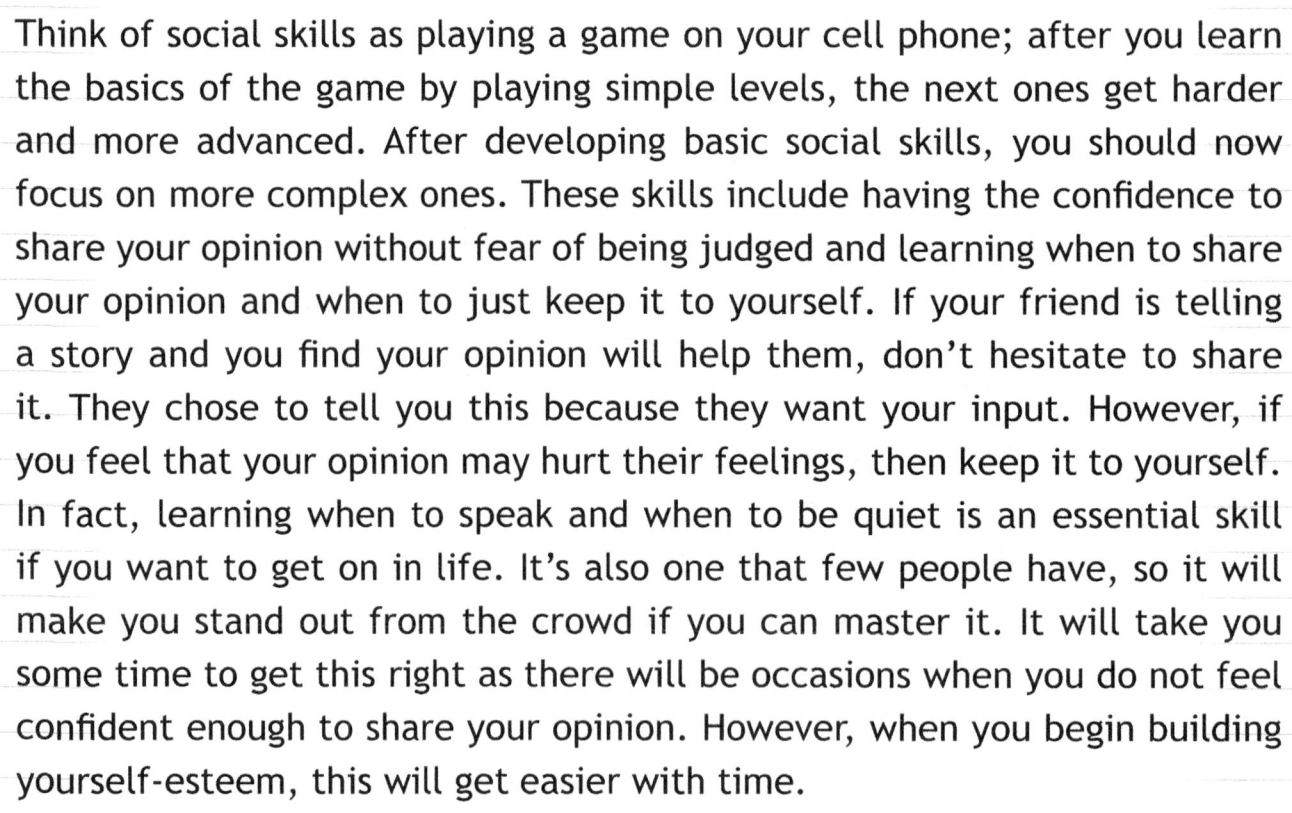

Think of social skills as playing a game on your cell phone; after you learn the basics of the game by playing simple levels, the next ones get harder and more advanced. After developing basic social skills, you should now focus on more complex ones. These skills include having the confidence to share your opinion without fear of being judged and learning when to share your opinion and when to just keep it to yourself. If your friend is telling a story and you find your opinion will help them, don't hesitate to share it. They chose to tell you this because they want your input. However, if you feel that your opinion may hurt their feelings, then keep it to yourself. In fact, learning when to speak and when to be quiet is an essential skill if you want to get on in life. It's also one that few people have, so it will make you stand out from the crowd if you can master it. It will take you some time to get this right as there will be occasions when you do not feel confident enough to share your opinion. However, when you begin building yourself-esteem, this will get easier with time.

This set of skills also includes a very important qualification: the ability to apologize. It takes courage and confidence to be accountable, own up to your mistakes, and say sorry. There is nothing wrong with apologizing; it shows your friends that you care about their feelings. Remember, apologizing shows character. Anytime you mistake or hurt someone's feelings, apologize immediately. Don't be uncool and let your pride get in the way. Many people have lost friends and even family members because they were too stubborn to say these three simple words "I am sorry." Apologizing will save your friendships.

Another life lesson you need to develop is to know when to ask for help. You may think asking your teacher or friend to help you with a math problem will make them think you aren't smart enough. However, this is the total opposite. Asking for help shows guts and that you are willing to learn. Being assertive is another great trait that you should work on developing. Stand up for yourself when one of your classmates bullies you. Be confident and understand that only weak people with low self-esteem enjoy bullying others. This is easier said than done, but when you learn how to build your self-esteem later in the book, you will have the courage to stand up for yourself and others. Working on your advanced social skills will take time and effort, but it will be worth it once you master them.

Emotional Social Skills

Being empathetic toward other people's feelings is a great skill that will make you become your friends' comfort zone, the one they go to whenever they have a problem because no one else will understand them better than you. Empathy is when you can understand and feel what the other person is feeling. If you are an empath, you will find yourself sympathizing when someone is sad and feeling joy when someone is happy. Although their happiness or sadness doesn't impact your life, you can still connect with them on a deeper level and feel their emotions. If you have this rare gift, nourish it and don't run away from it, as it will help you develop genuine friendships.

Emotional and social skills also include expressing your feelings freely without any shame. If you are sad, angry, or happy, don't shy away from showing these feelings. However, expressing your feelings doesn't mean you should be mean or hurtful to other people just because you are angry or having a bad day. You do this calmly by telling the other person how you feel or how their actions have hurt you. For instance, if your best friend said something the other day that you felt was inconsiderate, instead of avoiding them in school or just being mean for no reason, sit with them after school and tell them that their words hurt your feelings. In most cases, you'll probably find your friend wasn't aware that their actions were hurt-

ful, and they will apologize immediately. Expressing emotions will help you develop healthy relationships and behavior.

The Benefits of Having Good Social Skills

- Making you more self-aware
- Experience less bullying
- Developing effective communication skills with people your age and adults as well
- Feel safer at school
- Teaches you to work in a team
- Makes your school experience more comfortable
- Helps you achieve your goals
- Improves your listening skills
- Helps you be more in control of your emotions

Lack of Social Skills

Just like social skills have many benefits, a lack of these skills can cause you some grief in your social life.
- You will find yourself talking too much during social situations
- Feeling awkward and unsure about yourself, so you avoid social situations or withdraw from conversations
- You may have trouble understanding sarcasm or when someone tries to make a joke
- You will not be a good listener, which can affect your friendships
- You may share information with others using inappropriate methods like gossiping
- You will not be able to read facial cues and recognize when someone is embarrassed or upset

Quiz

You know enough by now about social skills so let's take a quiz to test yours. Just mark "yes" to the questions that apply to you, "sometimes" to the things that you struggle a little with, and "no" to the things that don't apply to you.

1. **Do you make eye contact when you talk to people?**
   - ☐ Yes
   - ☐ Sometimes
   - ☐ No

2. **Do you address people with their names? (As opposed to using bro, girlfriend, or dude).**
   - ☐ Yes
   - ☐ Sometimes
   - ☐ No

3. **Do you ask people questions that show genuine interest in their lives?**
   - ☐ Yes
   - ☐ Sometimes
   - ☐ No

4. **Do you know how to read body language and facial expressions?**
   - ☐ Yes
   - ☐ Sometimes
   - ☐ No

5. **Do you really listen to others without zoning out or making interruptions?**
   - ☐ Yes
   - ☐ Sometimes
   - ☐ No

6. Are you able to feel empathy?
- ☐ Yes
- ☐ Sometimes
- ☐ No

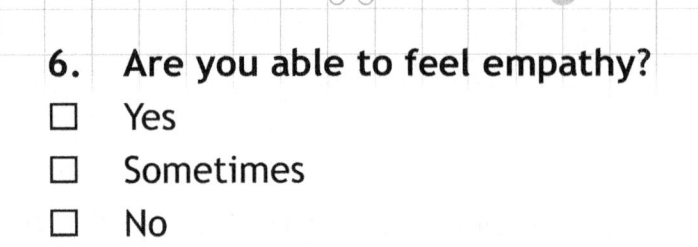

If you answer "yes" to all these questions, you have good social skills; if you answer "sometimes" to all or most of them, you are halfway there. However, if you answer "no" to all or most of these questions, don't fret; you have just begun your journey. In the coming chapters, you will learn more abilities that will help you master social skills.

Chapter 2 — Who Are Tweens?

The term "tween" refers to an age group of kids who are no longer kids but not yet teenagers. Tweens are typically middle-schoolers who are nearing puberty. They face many of the challenges that adolescents face, so if this is where you are, you can call yourself a tween.

You will probably be going through several physical and social changes. This is the beginning of you starting mature in a physical, mental, social, and emotional sense. You could also struggle to adjust to more responsibilities at home and school.

These changes are seen mostly by your parents and yourself. Parents notice that their kids are no longer little. However, they know their kids still need guidance in several areas of life. Tweens may feel somewhat confused and misunderstood, particularly because they're too old to be children and too young to be teenagers.

Being a tween comes with several challenges. You start learning more about the world around you and want to be more independent. You start building up your social skills and having your own ideas about things. However, as much as you don't want to believe it, you still need help when it comes to taking on the challenges.

Each age group and developmental stage comes with its own name, description, and characteristics. Unfortunately, as a tween, you're in a group that parents and other grown-ups find difficult to identify. This is because kids at this age grow and develop at their own pace and experience varying emotional, physical, and social changes. Tweens are one of the most diverse age groups that exist.

After reading this chapter, you'll understand who you are and what your folks know about you. This chapter will also touch on the changes you'll experience as a pre-teen. You'll also come across a questionnaire to help you better know yourself.

Tweens

The word "tween" comes from the combination of the words "between" and "teenager." This is because kids who fall into this age group refuse to be identified as children but are still younger than teenagers. The exact age group of tweens varies from one place to the next. However, tweens are generally believed to be any age between 9 and 12.

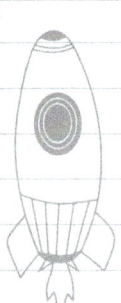

Even though tweens are considered a stand-alone age group, you are not often defined as a developmental stage. This is because children aged 9 to 12 have different rates of development. This term is relatively new because it was initially created for marketing purposes. It has grown in popularity in the past few years. Tweens are also referred to as pre-teens and middle-schoolers.

Challenges Tweens Face

Although tweens are not yet adolescents, which is a developmental stage notorious for its challenges, as a tween, you'll still face several obstacles in your social and personal lives. This is because your bodies are preparing to undergo huge changes as you age and approach puberty.

At this age, tweens also get exposed to shady behaviors and peer pressure. If you're a tween, you may feel pressured to try risky things so you can fit in. It's natural to feel curious about trying new things. However, if any of your friends try to pressure you into doing something that you think is risky, it's always best to take a step back and think before you jump into something that's not cool.

20

Another obstacle with being a tween is the sudden surge of homework. As you grow up, the number of assignments you have will increase. Don't be afraid to ask for help when needed- it can be hard to adjust to this sudden change. Search for tips and seek out guidance on how you can instill good study habits. The academic efforts that you start doing now will stick with you for a lifetime.

With the tween years comes a great deal of responsibilities. You may feel quite overwhelmed if you play a sport, do other extracurricular activities, or help out with chores at home. This is why good time-management habits must become part of your life. Make use of to-do lists and personalized schedules, and always remember that time is one of the most valuable assets you own. Aim to make every minute count. This doesn't mean you should bite off more than you can chew- this will only burn you out. Taking time to relax, binge-watch your favorite show, or just hang out with your friends.

The transition from elementary to middle school itself can be terrifying. Everything, from the academic structure, and the daily schedules to the curricula, are all different. This change can be difficult to adapt to, and the new information can be hard to grasp.

Unfortunately, many tweens also get into a lot of trouble with their friends, family, and children. The problem is that your age group struggles with difficult mood swings. It can sometimes feel like you're alone and no one understands you.

Changes During Tweens Years

Physical Changes

The mental, social, and physical changes that occur during your tween years are huge. For instance, dramatic changes happen in your brain's development. Boys will start experiencing growth spurts as they enter puberty at around 11 years old, which causes numerous quick changes. Girls also enter puberty at around 12 years old. Some girls even experience it as early as 8 or 9 years old.

Cognitive Changes

As you grow older, your brain functions will mature as well. At this point, you will start to grasp the consequences of your actions. Use this as an opportunity to think hard before you make any decisions. Take the time to weigh out the pros and cons of any situation and build your opinions based on real factors. Try to understand how other people think and consider why they may think, feel, and act the way they do. If you don't want people to treat you like a child, approach them like adults.

Emotional Changes

Being a pre-teen means you've also started picking up on your emotions and feelings. You're also beginning to view the world from a realistic perspective. Your tweens are when you begin exploring the things that matter in life and developing your own values and morals. It can be scary at first but don't hesitate to discuss your fears with a trusted adult.

Social Changes

You'll also come under a lot of social pressure to fit in. Middle school is among the most common places where bullying takes place. Tweens have to deal with the fact that they're moving to a much larger school with different social and educational expectations. Middle schoolers are under pressure to form new friend groups. This means you either have to find people you get along with or try to change your actions to be good enough to hang out with the cool kids.

As a tween, you become exposed to new people with different mindsets. You're still learning, which is why you shouldn't expect to get things right every time. You will eventually make mistakes and deal with people who don't have your best interests at heart. While this can be painful, it will add to your experiences in life. Think of your tween years as an opportunity to prepare yourself for adolescence and, eventually, adulthood.

Sense of Identity

As you were growing up, your actions and behaviors were mostly shaped by your parents and family members. You looked to them for guidance in every part of your life. For instance, if your dad is into baseball, you probably cheered for the same team as them without questioning. However, now that you're growing up, you may start to watch more games and cheer for a different team.

This is when you start exploring your passions and hobbies. Your parents may have signed you up for ballet when you were little, but a few years later, you discovered that you're truly passionate about something different, like soccer or horse riding. You may even give up sports entirely to focus on your newly found love for painting.

Your tweens are when you begin to form a sense of identity. It may feel very confusing at first because you will go through numerous stages before you get to the person you truly are. You'll still get influenced by your friend's and family's interests and change your clothing and music styles multiple times along the way, but that's fine because it allows you to discover what you like, what you don't like, and what you feel neutral about. You may feel lost and frustrated sometimes, but it helps to remind yourself that this is a normal part of growing up.

Embrace these changes as long as you're not doing anything that may harm you or anyone else. This experience is crucial to the person you'll become. You'll spend your tweens and teenage years jumping from hobby to hobby and changing your mind and styles a million times until you become the person you're meant to be as an adult.

Your Relationship with Your Parents Can Change

As a tween, it's normal to feel like you want more space and independence. As cliche as it sounds, you must understand that your parents will always be protective of you, no matter how old you grow. This can create issues between you and your parents.

If you want space, you may become less physically affectionate towards your parents. You may also feel like you don't want to answer any questions about your personal life. You may also feel pissed whenever they try to give you advice.

In reality, you need to accept that whether you're 5 or 24 years old, you'll always be a child in your parents' eyes. They always think they know what's best for you, even if you have a different opinion. They can feel overbearing, but you should remind yourself that you'll always need them in life. Nothing compares to the love and compassion of a supportive parent.

Potential Interests

Being a tween is all about finding the right balance in life, which can be difficult to do when everything, from your thoughts, feelings, and physical appearance to your friends, responsibilities, and school, is changing. You can be stuck between not wanting to grow up and dying to be a proper teenager. This is something that everyone all over the world goes through, and it often helps to understand what people your age normally do. Learning about the interests of other pre-teens can give you ideas about what you can do in your free time, give you insight into what other people your age are doing, and may even help you realize that you aren't alone!

Watching Television and Playing Video Games

Tweens typically spend most of their time either binge-watching their favorite television shows or playing video games. TVs and tablets are considered the main entertainment sources for anyone aged 9 to 12. Whether you're watching Slugterra or Yu-Gi-Oh, animated TV shows are probably on your most-watched list. The average pre-teen spends around 2 hours of their day watching television.

Being Active Online

Many tweens enjoy being active on their social media accounts and watching online videos. Smartphones have become an essential aspect of our lives. The chances are that you need your phone for school as well. It's how you communicate with your friends to prepare for group assignments and how you google information if you need it for your homework. If your friends are still not big on social media, you will likely spend most of your time watching TV. Make sure you're using social media safely, as all users, both children, and adults, are always at risk of cyberbullying, phishing, and other online dangers.

Reading

Reading never gets old. Nothing beats curling up in your bed and allowing the words and pages to transport you to fantastical places and stories only real in your imagination. Around 50% of pre-teens must read for educational purposes, which is why many of them shy away from doing it for fun. You may be surprised to learn that many tweens still like to read in their free time. You can give genres like comedy and fantasy a go since they're the most popular among your age group.

Questionnaire: Get to Know Yourself Better!

Answering the following questionnaire can help you learn a lot about yourself. This will help you set out on the path to self-discovery and can ultimately help you shape your unique sense of self.

Keep your answers in a safe place, and feel free to return to this questionnaire and update your answers whenever you need to. Make sure to think deeply about what you write each time, compare it to your past answers, and account for everything that has changed. Take the time to think about why you've come up with different answers and why you felt the need to update your questionnaire. If you feel compelled enough to write about your new revelations, these are likely big changes worth thinking about.

The answers to your questions should be as long, short, detailed, or brief as you want. The more honest you are, the more you will learn about yourself. You don't need to share your answers with anyone if you don't wish to.

1. What do you believe your strengths are?
   _____
   _____
   _____

2. What are your goals for this school year?
   _____
   _____
   _____

3. If you had the option to move to any city, state, or country in the world, where would that be? Why did you choose this place?
   _____
   _____
   _____

4. Is there anyone who you talk to whenever you have a problem? If not, why? If you do, then how do they help you?
   _____
   _____
   _____

5. Are you worried about anything at the moment? What is it?
   _____
   _____
   _____

6. What are the things that you enjoy doing for fun?
   _____
   _____
   _____

7. What do you want your parents to know about you? How do they make you feel misunderstood if they do?
   _____
   _____
   _____

8. Do your friends or classmates make you feel misunderstood? What's something you wish they knew about you?
   _____
   _____
   _____

9. Where do you feel most at peace? Where do you feel the safest?
   _____
   _____
   _____

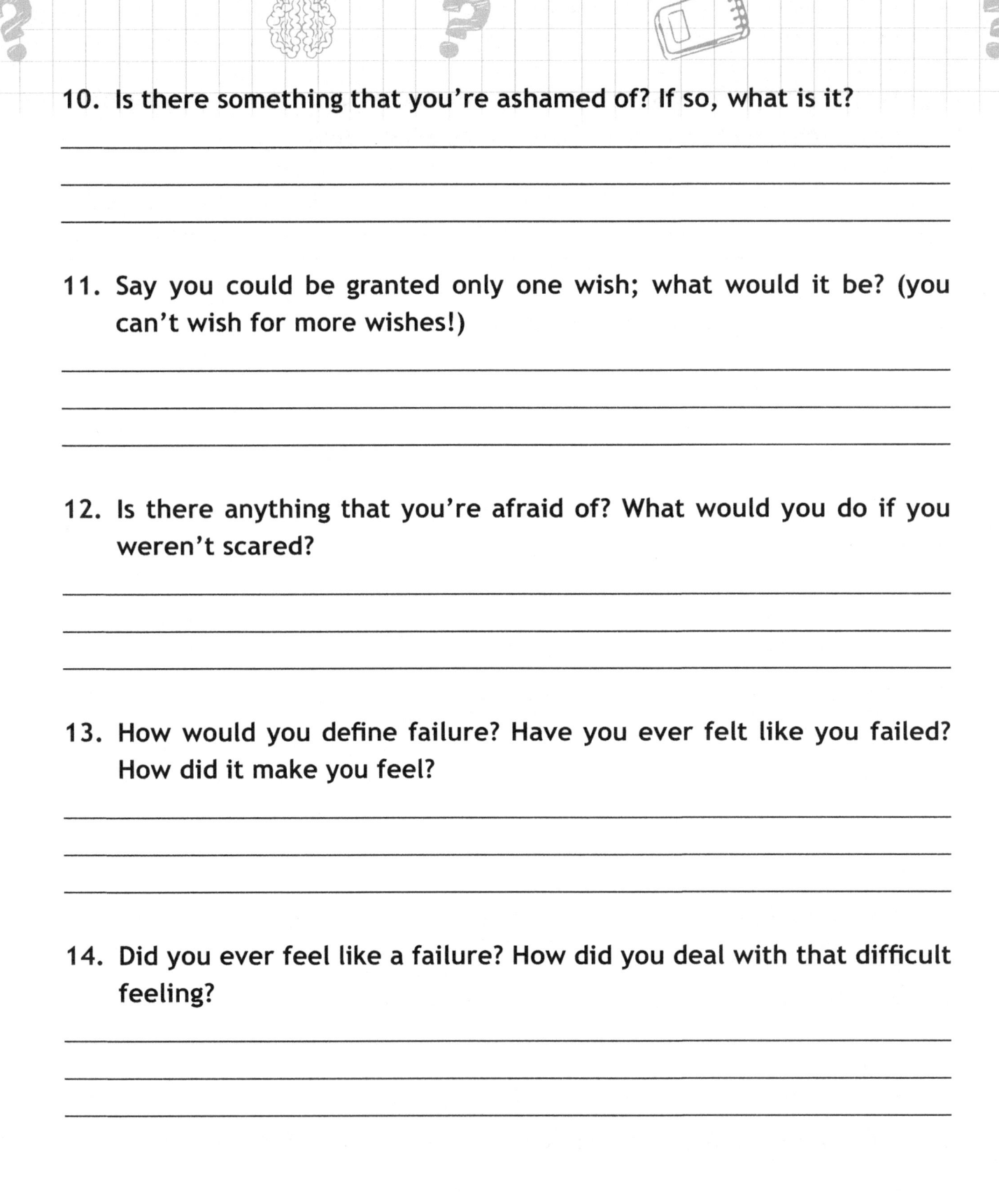

10. Is there something that you're ashamed of? If so, what is it?
___
___
___

11. Say you could be granted only one wish; what would it be? (you can't wish for more wishes!)
___
___
___

12. Is there anything that you're afraid of? What would you do if you weren't scared?
___
___
___

13. How would you define failure? Have you ever felt like you failed? How did it make you feel?
___
___
___

14. Did you ever feel like a failure? How did you deal with that difficult feeling?
___
___
___

15. Do you sometimes feel like you're different from those around you? Why?
___
___
___

16. What makes you unique?
___
___
___

17. Did anything that an adult said ever stick with you? This could be positive or negative. Do you think that what they said is correct?
___
___
___

18. How do you react, and what do you do if you think someone doesn't like you?
___
___
___

19. What is something that you've accomplished and are very proud of?
___
___
___

20. State everything that comes to your mind that you can control in life.
___
___

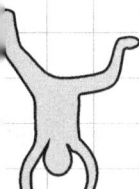

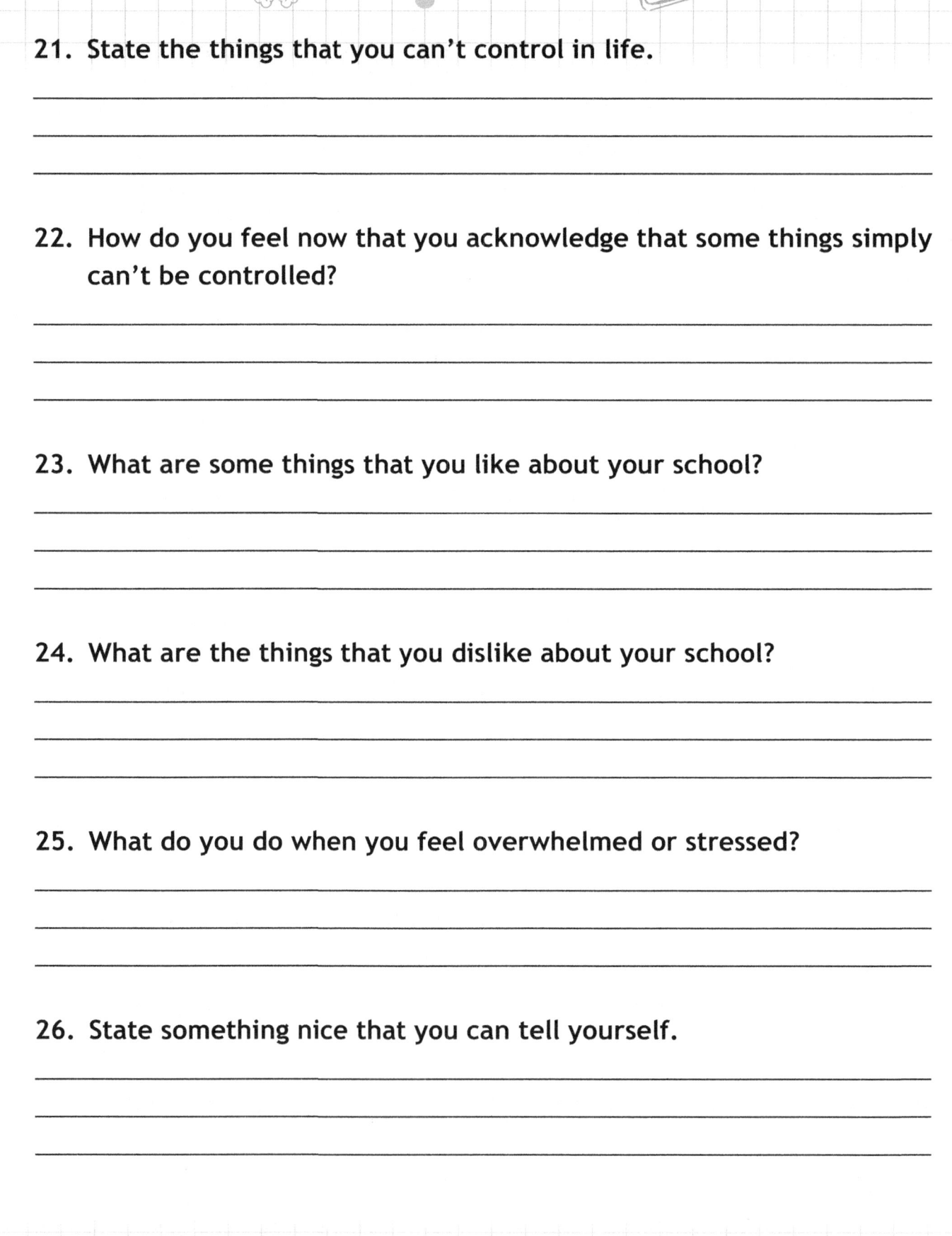

21. State the things that you can't control in life.
___
___
___

22. How do you feel now that you acknowledge that some things simply can't be controlled?
___
___
___

23. What are some things that you like about your school?
___
___
___

24. What are the things that you dislike about your school?
___
___
___

25. What do you do when you feel overwhelmed or stressed?
___
___
___

26. State something nice that you can tell yourself.
___
___
___

27. Recall the happiest memory you have.
_____
_____
_____

28. What do you do whenever you're feeling down?
_____
_____
_____

29. Do you think that it's okay to cry?
_____
_____
_____

30. Do you believe it's okay to yell if you're angry or down?
_____
_____
_____

31. Do you have a favorite book? What is it?
_____
_____
_____

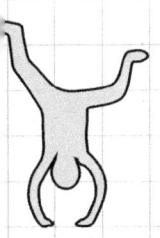

32. What's something that you can eat and never get bored of?
_____
_____
_____

33. What's your favorite color? Can you think of a reason why you chose this color?
_____
_____
_____

34. Do you have a favorite band?
_____
_____
_____

35. What's your favorite animal?
_____
_____
_____

36. What are you thankful for in life?
_____
_____
_____

37. What do you like about yourself?
_____
_____
_____

You are not a child anymore, yet, you're still not old enough to be a teenager. This can be very confusing. You may feel pressured to follow everyone's pace when it comes to growing up. However, you need to remind yourself that you are unique. Your feelings are valid, but a very important part of maturing is knowing how to deal with your emotions.

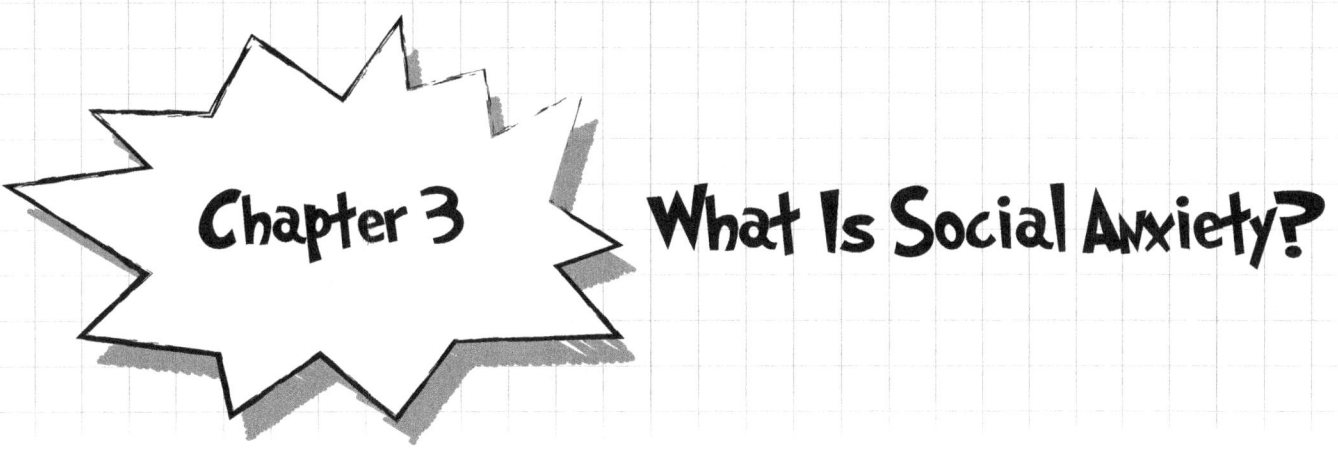

Chapter 3: What Is Social Anxiety?

In this chapter, you'll understand everything that you need to know about social anxiety disorder. You'll find out what it is, the symptoms that go with it, as well as what causes it. You'll learn how to deal with someone who struggles with social anxiety and whether or not you can be successful if you're socially anxious. Finally, a self-assessment questionnaire can help you determine whether you get anxious in social settings.

What Is Social Anxiety Disorder?

People who struggle with social anxiety disorders usually feel anxious and jittery in certain social situations. These feelings of uneasiness could be caused by a fear of rejection, potential awkwardness, embarrassment, and negative judgment. It's normal to feel anxious in some social situations, like giving a presentation or participating in a large performance, but social anxiety disorders are very intense. The fear and worry can get to the point where the sufferer's personal life is affected. If you or someone else has had these symptoms for more than six months, they likely have this condition.

Socially anxious people may try to mask their physical symptoms. In addition to feeling worried about the social situation, they're also worried about appearing shaky, trembling, or blushing, as well as feeling and looking sick, sweating, and having an increased heart rate. These are some of the more intense symptoms of social anxiety disorder. People with it think that these physical symptoms make them come across as unintelligent, annoying, or awkward.

People with anxiety usually know that their fears are irrational and incredibly excessive. However, they still can't help being overwhelmed by these emotions. It can also seem impossible to shut the intrusive thoughts down and keep their feelings under wraps. People with social anxiety react most worriedly when meeting new people, having to perform or present in front of others, and being called to speak in front of many people. Even when they're out with their friends, people with social anxiety may feel distressed if they realize they're the center of attention for a moment. Normal daily activities, such as eating or drinking in front of anyone, talking to a cashier or putting their money away after paying at a store, using a public restroom, or talking to anyone about academics or school, can trigger the affected person's social anxiety.

Unfortunately, many people with social anxiety think this disorder is merely a part of their personality. They think that how they feel, think, and act is just a product of excessive shyness, which is why they don't seek professional help. However, this is not the case.

Social Anxiety vs. Shyness

Unlike social anxiety, shyness is a part of your personality and doesn't need to be treated. It is usually happening and is more visible than social anxiety. People usually feel shy when they meet new people or find themselves in new situations. However, they start feeling more comfortable once they adapt to the situation. Even though social anxiety may also be situational for some people, the worry often occurs way before the event starts, during, and after it ends. Since this is a mental disorder, leaving it untreated can cause it to worsen over time. Even though the affected people are incredibly worried, they may be confident and extroverted.

Symptoms of Social Anxiety Disorder

Social anxiety disorder impacts individuals on the physical, emotional, and mental levels. It affects the way that the affected person feels, thinks, and behaves, as well as their overall physical health.

The following are some symptoms that accompany social anxiety:

- Nausea, blushing, trembling, increased heart rate, and sweating are among the physical symptoms a person may experience.
- Their judgment may be off, or they have a blank mind.
- Feeling panicky and experiencing panic attacks.
- Feeling afraid of appearing anxious in front of others or feeling anxious in general.
- Dreading social situations, especially when meeting new people.
- Feeling incredibly fearful of being subject to negative judgment.
- Experiencing speaking difficulties.
- Having a rigid posture and maintaining a soft tone and voice during social interactions.
- Finding it difficult to maintain eye contact with others.
- Feeling embarrassed for doing normal things and being extremely self-conscious in public.
- Being very sensitive to criticism.
- Having issues with self-esteem and engaging in self-deprecating talk.
- Going to great lengths to avoid situations that may trigger anxiety.

These are all things that can upset the flow of your daily life. The symptoms of social anxiety can get in the way of your school life and academics. If you let it overpower you, you may not be able to reach your full potential. This is because severe anxiety may stop you from engaging in group school projects or presenting your assignments with pride in front of everyone. Chronic social anxiety disorder can result in depression and other mental health conditions.

When kids struggle with social anxiety, the symptoms may flare up at any time in any situation, whether with adults or other kids. Anxiety in small children can show up as crying, tantrums, shrinking, freezing, clinging to their caretakers, or staying silent in social situations.

Causes of Social Anxiety

Social anxiety can be a result of a broad range of issues. However, the most common causes include:

- **Past Traumas and Life Challenges:** Things that happened in the past put extraordinary stress or trauma on the sufferer. Examples of these events commonly include chronic illnesses, the death of someone close, violence, or abuse. If your friend has been rejected or left out, bullied, or humiliated, this may be why they're struggling with social anxiety disorder.
- **Genetics:** Like many mental and physical health conditions, anxiety disorders can be hereditary. This means they can be passed off from a parent to their child.
- **Parenting Styles:** Someone who is brought up in an extremely overprotective or guarded environment may develop a social anxiety disorder.

Dealing with Someone with Social Anxiety

At first glance, you may think it's hard and frightening to deal with someone with social anxiety. However, you'll be surprised that their symptoms can become more manageable if you take the time to understand and support them. Here are some things you can do when dealing with someone who struggles with social anxiety:

Be Patient

Dealing with anxiety can be extremely tiring. The treatment process is extensive, as well. It can cause someone with a mental health condition to adopt new behavioral and thinking patterns, so try your best not to become frustrated with how they act. Be patient and supportive and validate their thoughts no matter how irrational they may be.

Understand Their Feelings

Sometimes, people get anxious for no apparent reason. Instead of focusing on the why consider the how. Ask them how they're feeling and ask them to explain their symptoms. If they wish, they could write them down. Don't ask them too many questions, and don't deny their feeling. Avoid using words like "stop feeling scared" or "there's no reason to feel this anxious"? They probably already know that they're overreacting. Instead, create a safe space where they can freely release all the pressure they've been experiencing.

Avoid Being Critical

Anxious people are already overly self-critical. They also think that everyone is watching and judging their every action. They always worry about their posture, clothes, and appearance and repeatedly think about their words before speaking up. Even then, they may beat themselves up for saying the wrong thing or coming off as awkward. Criticizing your anxious friend's behaviors will only make things worse for them. Don't tell your friend that they're too uptight or quiet because they'll obsess over your words. Don't expect more than what they can offer at the moment. Trying to keep one's anxious thoughts at bay is already hard as is.

Try to Distract Them

The right distractions can help shift your friend's mind off intrusive thoughts for a few minutes. Ask them if they'd like to play their favorite video game, watch a movie, visit a bookstore, or go for a walk whenever they notice that their anxiety is flaring up. You can also help them put together a customized anxiety kit. Include things that can help calm them down or distract them whenever needed.

Help Them Put Their Thoughts into Perspective
Anxiety results in clouded judgment and makes it difficult to think clearly. They need someone to knock some sense into them and shift their focus onto the bigger picture. Ask them questions such as "what's the worst that could happen?" "What is the most rational outcome?" "What are all the good things that could happen?" "When was the last time you experienced this type of anxiety? It passed. Didn't it?" "Will this matter in a few years or even months?"

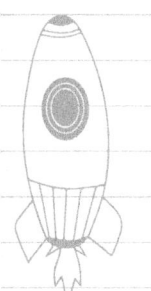

Get Them to Stop Hiding
This can be incredibly hard. However, the only way someone can overcome their anxiety is by coming face to face with their triggers. Encourage your friend to stop avoiding social situations and tell them that you'll be right there to help them stay grounded for however long they need you. You don't even need to start big. If they've been self-isolating, call a friend or family member and ask them to get in touch with your friend. Then, encourage them to meet up with their closest friends in a non-crowded area until they're ready to make it to larger outings and events.

Stay Positive
Completing normal day-to-day tasks can be an incredible milestone for people who struggle with mental health conditions. Some depressed individuals feel successful whenever they make their beds. Eating breakfast is an incredible step forward for people who struggle with certain types of eating disorders. Similarly, getting in touch with an old friend can feel like quite the achievement for someone with a social anxiety disorder. Although these are all things you probably do daily with ease, individuals with mental disorders struggle with them all the time. This is why it's important to acknowledge every little milestone your friend hits. Recognize their progress and give them positive feedback.

Ask Them to Consider Treatment

Discuss with your friend all the potential benefits they may experience once they seek professional help. Explain that you'd be glad to help them find someone whom they can trust. If they're not open to this idea, ask them why. Listen to their concerns and explain why they may be wrong. You can help them book a doctor's appointment, enroll them in a self-help program, or search for a support group they can join.

Can You Be Successful if You're Socially Anxious?

Anyone can succeed if they want to, even with social anxiety. You and how you see your anxiety is the only thing that can ever get between you and your success. You get to choose whether your mental condition blocks your potential. If you tell yourself that you can't do this, that, or succeed in life because you're socially anxious, then you might as well never leave your bed.

If you visit a mental health professional, they may discuss the possibility of taking medications, depending on your condition. Whether you decide to take them is up to you and your guardians. While these medications can help you keep your intrusive thoughts under control, some people don't like depending on an external source. In that case, they work with their therapists to find ways to help them deal with their anxiety themselves. Whenever you step out of the house and feel your intrusive thoughts start washing over you, it helps to tell yourself how you want your life to be. Imagine the person you wish to be in the future, and go into as much detail as possible. Then, ask yourself one question: "will I be able to achieve that if I allow anxiety to get in the way?" Your answer will be "no" every time. You will not amount to anything if you constantly worry about what people think of you. You will never be everyone's cup of tea, and you must make peace with this fact.

You can be successful even if you don't manage to overcome your social anxiety. Here's a little trick that you can use: play pretend. If you play the part, just like in the movies, is the situation in question really happening? No. Everything is planned. You're playing your part according to a script. Create a character of your choice and give it all the characteristics and traits you desire. Take on this role and go on about your life. Doing so can help you see things through a much clearer lens. It can give you more control, confidence, and a better outlook and perspective.

Self-Assessment:
Do I Struggle with Social Anxiety Disorder?

Answering this quiz can help you work out whether you get anxious in social situations or not. But, you need to know that this questionnaire is not a substitute for proper diagnosis by a doctor. Mental health conditions, including social anxiety disorder, can only be diagnosed by a mental health professional.

Either way, taking this quiz can help you understand whether you need to do something about getting some professional help. Many people who struggle with mental disorders worry that their symptoms are not concerning enough to seek the intervention of a specialist, which is why this quiz can be a great step toward receiving the needed treatment.

1. Do social situations make you feel anxious and give rise to feelings of panic?
   - ☐ Yes, this happens often
   - ☐ Yes, this happens sometimes
   - ☐ No, this rarely happens
   - ☐ No, this never happens

2. Do you worry about how other people will think about you?
   - ☐ Yes, this happens often
   - ☐ Yes, this happens sometimes
   - ☐ No, this rarely happens
   - ☐ No, this never happens

3. Do these worries make you afraid that someone may think badly of you?
   - ☐ Yes, this happens often
   - ☐ Yes, this happens sometimes
   - ☐ No, this rarely happens
   - ☐ No, this never happens

4. Are these fears and feelings of anxiety strong enough to make you stay away from social situations?
   ☐ Yes, this happens often
   ☐ Yes, this happens sometimes
   ☐ No, this rarely happens
   ☐ No, this never happens

5. If you find yourself in a situation where you have to interact with people you don't know well, would this make you feel extremely uncomfortable?
   ☐ Yes, this happens often
   ☐ Yes, this happens sometimes
   ☐ No, this rarely happens
   ☐ No, this never happens

6. Would these feelings of discomfort be enough to make you miss out on the situation, gathering, or event?
   ☐ Yes, this happens often
   ☐ Yes, this happens sometimes
   ☐ No, this rarely happens
   ☐ No, this never happens

7. Do you panic if there's something that you need to do around other people even though you're competent in that area?
   ☐ Yes, this happens often
   ☐ Yes, this happens sometimes
   ☐ No, this rarely happens
   ☐ No, this never happens

8. Do you feel anxious when presenting, speaking, or participating in a performance in front of a group of people?
   - ☐ Yes, this happens often
   - ☐ Yes, this happens sometimes
   - ☐ No, this rarely happens
   - ☐ No, this never happens

9. Do you find yourself thinking that other people think that you're weak, annoying, anxious, disheveled, stupid, incompetent, unlikeable, or intimidating?
   - ☐ Yes, this happens often
   - ☐ Yes, this happens sometimes
   - ☐ No, this rarely happens
   - ☐ No, this never happens

10. Do you find yourself worrying that your anxiety is showing? Do you constantly check for signs like trembling, shaking, blushing, inaccurate wording, or staring in fear that anyone else notices them?
    - ☐ Yes, this happens often
    - ☐ Yes, this happens sometimes
    - ☐ No, this rarely happens
    - ☐ No, this never happens

11. Are you unusually conscious and careful around other people? Do you constantly think about how you will act or what you will say for fear of being rejected, coming off as awkward, embarrassing yourself, or offending anyone?
    - ☐ Yes, this happens often
    - ☐ Yes, this happens sometimes
    - ☐ No, this rarely happens
    - ☐ No, this never happens

12. Do you worry excessively about upcoming social situations? Are these worries overstated compared to the actual threats of a triggering situation?
    - ☐ Yes, this happens often
    - ☐ Yes, this happens sometimes
    - ☐ No, this rarely happens
    - ☐ No, this never happens

13. Do you think your anxiety affects your academic, school, and home life? Does it get in the way of your friendships?
    - ☐ Yes, this happens often
    - ☐ Yes, this happens sometimes
    - ☐ No, this rarely happens
    - ☐ No, this never happens

At its core, social anxiety disorder is a mental health condition that is characterized by extreme worry and fear of being judged and embarrassed in social situations. People who struggle with severe social anxiety may self-isolate to avoid social interactions. This may result in additional mental disorders like depression.

Chapter 4: Boosting Self-Esteem and Confidence

An individual's self-esteem and confidence play a central role in their social performance, which is even more valid for you if you are a pre-teen or tween. Pre-adolescents often have self-esteem issues, making it really hard to interact socially in school or other gatherings. At this age, you are going through countless changes in your life, from physical changes to hormonal ones. And this can make you feel vulnerable and extra sensitive, which is the root cause of low self-confidence and esteem issues.

So, before developing decent social skills, it's crucial to understand how to tackle these feelings of self-doubt and boost your self-confidence. This chapter will explain why you may have developed self-esteem issues and what you can do to boost your self-confidence.

Self-Esteem Defined

While you most likely have a good idea about it, the first step to learning about self-esteem is understanding what it is exactly. Self-esteem can be defined as a person's sense of self-worth. It is used to measure how much a person values themselves. It can also be defined as your attitude towards yourself. Many things influence it, such as:

- Personality
- Life experiences
- Appearance
- Intellectual capability
- Genetics

- Health
- Age
- Social standing
- Other people's behaviors
- Comparisons

Self-esteem is not something that is fixed, rigid, or never changes. It is flexible when worked upon. This is good news and should give you the courage to work on yourself and your confidence levels instead of accepting defeat and staying hopeless. An individual's personality is directly linked with their self-esteem; for instance, people with high self-esteem are more confident and have strong personalities. On the other hand, people with low self-esteem have drab personalities. So, by working on your personality, you can improve your self-esteem. Some other concepts associated with self-esteem include:

Self-Esteem vs. Self-Concept

Many people confuse self-esteem with self-concept, even though they are two separate notions. Self-concept is an awareness of oneself, weaknesses, tendencies, habits, preferences, and skills. The main difference between the two ideas is other people's opinions about you in addition to your own.

Self-Esteem vs. Self-Image

Another similar term that people often confuse self-esteem with is self-image. This term has a similar meaning to self-concept and generally refers to how you see yourself. However, it can give you false thoughts about yourself, either positively or negatively. Your self-image can be far from reality, and although it is an important aspect of self-esteem, it does not define you completely.

Self-Esteem vs. Self-Confidence

Self-esteem is not the same thing as self-confidence either. Self-confidence is about being able to trust your abilities, how you can deal with challenges, and how well you can solve problems. It doesn't have anything to do with the stuff inside you; that is about your self-esteem; it's all about wanting other people to tell you you're great, and only then will you believe it. For instance, a person can have high self-confidence in a subject they're an expert in but overall lack self-esteem in other areas of their life.

Low Self-Esteem and Quality of Life

Having low self-esteem can suck and affect your life in a bad way. It affects your relationships, performance in life, and also your health. Research has linked low self-esteem with poor quality of life, as it can affect people's lives in different ways, like:

- Constantly feeling bad about yourself can make you angry, sad, depressed, guilty, ashamed, or anxious.
- Accepting toxic or bullying behavior from friends or peers. You may find it hard to believe that you deserve and have a right to be treated with love and respect. Thus, you're more likely to tolerate any kind of abusive or bullying behavior from the people around you.
- Avoid any new challenges or opportunities that might come your way. If you don't believe in your capabilities, you will be scared to take risks.
- Perfecting every task, no matter how much effort it requires. You may become an overachiever to make up for what you believe is inferiority.
- Avoiding people or social gatherings. You may feel self-conscious when participating in activities involving other people. You may be afraid others are judging you, even when it's unlikely.
- Not properly coping with a challenging life event because you already believe yourself to be hopeless; as a result, you find you're unable to face challenges that come your way.
- Lacking in self-care or excessive neglect of your health. You may be doing this because you have stopped caring about your well-being. In extreme cases, this can turn into substance abuse or other cases of extreme neglect.

Causes of Low Self-Esteem in Pre-Teens

Low self-esteem isn't something instinctive in everyone's personality. No, it's developed after unfortunate circumstances the person has been through. To work on your self-esteem issues, you first need to understand where these issues came from. Once you understand the root cause of your esteem issues, you can start working on eliminating the effects of these traumas and becoming a better version of yourself. For pre-teens, there can be many times when your self-esteem takes a hit. This is a time of extreme ups and downs, and as a result, you could end up storing this trauma in your mind. You might be suffering from poor self-esteem issues due to:

- Bad or abusive childhood experiences that may have left a scar on your developing mind. These events are usually traumatic and can often affect you deeply. Such instances can include neglect, abuse, violence, the death of a loved one, or the imprisonment of a family member. Less severe experiences could include verbal abuse, insufficient parental support, or bullying.
- Societal expectations from you can ruin your mental health and leave you unable to do even the simplest of tasks. As a pre-teen, you're probably constantly exposed to social media and the unrealistic standards of beauty and success you see there. This may force you to compare yourself to these unrealistic standards, and when you come up short, you feel like you are not good enough.
- Attacks on your identity can leave you feeling extremely self-conscious and weak in the eyes of others. Hurtful messages and comments about your race, sexuality, or standard can shake your pride. Those with physical ailments are also often a target of hate speech, leaving them unworthy of love.
- Jokes on your appearance can also make you feel self-conscious and result in you developing a poor self-image. Even if no one targets your appearance, self-made insecurities can make you feel vulnerable and

conscious of your physical looks. This can be especially hard to overcome since changing your appearance is not simple.
- Unsupportive parents can be the biggest cause of self-esteem issues that you may have. Parents often put their children down in the name of disciplining them without thinking about the way it affects their minds. Teachers and mentors can do the same with pre-teens and, thus, make you feel unloved or not worthy. Unrealistic academic expectations from parents also cause these problems. Not every child has the same level of intellect, and they should be handled with love and respect instead of forcing them to score well in class.

Signs of Low Self-Esteem

Poor self-esteem can deeply affect your personality, life, and performance. The signs of low self-esteem can sometimes be pretty apparent but are mostly subtle and not quite easy to detect. Identifying the signs of low self-esteem is another step towards eliminating your self-doubts and improving your self-confidence. However, they are not very easy to identify, as these signs can vary from person to person. For instance, someone with low self-esteem may talk negatively about themselves, while another person might be going out of their way to make others pleased with them. In either case, the importance of identifying these signs doesn't get reduced. Some common signs of poor self-esteem issues can include:

1. **Lack of Control**
   If you suffer from self-esteem issues, you probably think you have little to no control over what happens in your life. This is usually because you believe you are powerless against your problems and assume you don't have what it takes to solve them. High self-esteem makes the circumstances bearable for them even if someone doesn't have complete control of a situation.

2. **Negative Social Comparison**

   If you have low self-esteem issues, you will often find yourself doing "upward social comparison." This is where you compare yourself with people you think are better than you. This act itself is not just a sign of low self-esteem but is also extremely damaging to one's self-confidence and mental health.

3. **Problems Asking for Help**

   As a young teen struggling with low self-esteem, you can have trouble asking people for help. You may feel that you do not deserve help and shy away from troubling others, even if it is your right to do so. You may often feel embarrassed to ask for something, as you imagine others think you are incompetent.

4. **Worry and Self-Doubt**

   Another sign of low self-esteem is constant worrying and doubting yourself over every decision you make. If you struggle with low self-worth, you'll always find yourself fretting and obsessing about your choices. You may often doubt your own opinions and be comfortable sticking with others suggestions, even if you feel they're wrong.

5. **Trouble Accepting Positive Feedback**

   Suffering from low self-esteem can make you less likely to accept compliments from other people. This is because you don't believe any positive feedback comes your way. After all, you don't have a good opinion of yourself. This can also make you think the other person is being sarcastic or even cruel when making good comments about you.

6. **Negative Self-Talk**

   A poor self-image is what makes you keep your focus on your flaws instead of your strengths. Rather than being kind and accepting who you are, you amplify your flaws and practice negative self-talk most of the time. Whenever things go wrong, you often blame yourself for every little mistake, always finding a reason to believe it was your fault.

7. **Poor Outlook**

   People with low self-esteem often have pessimistic and miserable personalities, always seeing the worst in any situation. If you feel like there's little chance that the future will be better, you probably have this kind of outlook on life, and so you probably keep finding excuses not to make your life any better. You are also likely to self-sabotage your chances to move towards betterment.

8. **Lack of Boundaries**

   Creating healthy boundaries is something people learn during their early life. Children who were given a chance to create healthy boundaries are more likely to have high self-esteem. Whereas people with low self-esteem issues struggle to set clear boundaries. If you are too scared to drive people away by setting boundaries, you will likely end up with abusive partners or disrespectful relationships.

9. **Trying to Please Others**

   People pleasing is a common sign of low self-esteem. This is when you believe that external validation will help you feel better inside, but this is not actually true. Kids who do this will go overboard to make people happy with them, neglecting their own needs in the process. This habit also makes other people use them for their benefit, and they keep suffering in silence. Saying no is impossible for these people.

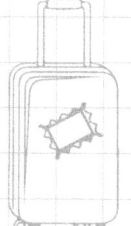

How to Improve Self-Esteem

The road to improvement starts with you; once you decide to change yourself, there's nothing that can stand in your way. While it can be difficult to get out of old habits, working on yourself, one step at a time, will ensure that you see progress. Improving your self-esteem is crucial to living a happy, healthy, and successful life. The process itself does not have to be complicated; here are some simple ways you can tackle your low self-esteem issues and improve your self-confidence.

1. Challenge Your Negative Beliefs

Your negative beliefs and pessimistic thinking make you miss out on good opportunities in life, so this is the first thing you need to change. You must first identify and challenge your negative beliefs to improve your self-image. Start by noticing any negative thoughts you might have about yourself. Isolate these thoughts and then think of reasons that prove them wrong. For instance, if you're thinking, "I have no friends," look for evidence that proves this statement wrong. Write it down, and whenever you're having this negative thought, go through this list of reasons again. Do this for every negative thought you have, and you'll be rid of these thoughts faster than you know.

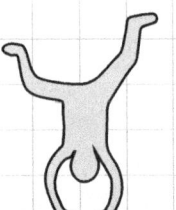

_____
_____
_____
_____
_____
_____
_____
_____

2. Count Your Blessings

The next step towards building self-esteem is finding positive things about yourself and your life. It's a good idea to write down whatever blessings you can think of. For instance, you could be good at sports or studies. Whatever it is, write it on your list, and look back at this list whenever you're feeling down or doubting yourself. Replace negative self-talk with positive internal dialogues to cheer you on. It's understandable if you sometimes revert to your old habits, but make sure you always catch yourself and put in more effort towards your well-being.

_____
_____
_____
_____
_____
_____
_____
_____
_____

3. Build Positive Relationships

The kind of people you surround yourself with has a big influence on how you feel about yourself. The people around you can either build you up or tear you down. Hanging out with negative, jealous, or toxic people will not help you feel good about yourself. Toxic people will take every gap to bring you down, and people you might consider to be your friends can turn out to be your worst enemies. They will pass comments and do things that will indirectly affect your self-esteem. The best thing you can do for yourself is to let these people go. Keep the people who make you feel good around you, people who are supportive and never try to bring you down.

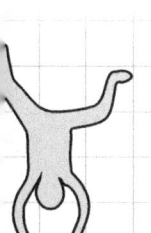

4. Take a Break

Know that it's okay to take a break. You don't have to be perfect every second of the day, and you're allowed to make mistakes. Trying to improve your self-esteem does not mean you will always feel good about yourself. Sometimes you might feel down, but don't let that fool you into thinking that you're hopeless. Avoid any kind of self-criticism in front of other people; this makes your self-esteem worse. Be kind to yourself and be self-compassionate.

5. Learn to Say No

A common sign of low self-esteem is not being able to say no to people who ask for favors. However, this is essential in this day and age of extreme mental pressure. While it might be hard for you to say no to people and stand up for yourself, you will have to do this one day or another. So, why not start right now? Develop your assertiveness and make yourself clear when you say no to someone. This will help you improve your self-esteem and reduce the burden you've put on yourself by saying yes to everyone.

6. Work on Your Physical Health

It is much easier to feel good about yourself when you're fit and healthy. Working on your physical body will go a long way to stop feeling self-conscious about your body. Try different exercises, diets, and other healthy habits to improve your lifestyle. This will not just help you boost your confidence but also make your overall lifestyle better.

In today's world, confidence is everything. Gone are the days when you could keep your head down and still become successful. Today's world is all about selling yourself, and you can only do this successfully when you're fully confident about yourself and have a high self-image. So, start working on yourself today by facing the problems holding you back and then by eliminating those problems.

Chapter 5 — Making Friends

If you watch reruns of the TV show Friends with your parents, know one thing, that the friendship between these six characters is nothing but genuine. The same goes for the kids on Stranger Things: Mike, Will, El, Lucas, Dustin, and Max. This group of friends will do anything for each other. They would even risk their lives for one another without thinking twice. It's true that in real life, people don't have to go to the Upside Down or face creatures from another dimension to prove how much you mean to them. However, a real friend should be there for you through thick and thin. Naturally, you love your friends so much that you are willing to forgive them or give them excuses for certain behavior. Everyone makes mistakes, and forgiveness is good quality. Still, you should know the difference between making mistakes and ill-intentioned behavior.

So, what is a "true friend"? What makes a friendship genuine? A true friend is someone you can count on because you know they will always have your back. They will stand up for you if someone hurts you, bullies you, or makes fun of you. It doesn't matter who it is; your friend will always defend you. Whenever you need them, they will be there for you no matter what. When you ask for their help, they will come running without expecting anything in return.

If someone says something negative about you behind your back, they will never repeat these words to you. A genuine friend will also make it clear that no one can say anything bad about you in front of them. They will never lie to you. They won't ever be fake or phony with you. They are always their truest selves around you; they never exaggerate their stuff to be cool in your eyes or deceive you into taking advantage of them. They trust you with all their secrets and are never afraid to be vulnerable around you. As a result of this mutual trust, they become your confidants and will never reveal your secrets. They will never hurt you with their words or actions and will say sorry immediately if this ever happens. If you ask them for their opinion about something, they won't hesitate to tell you the truth even if they know that you won't like it. A true friend is always by your side and will never leave. They love you and accept you for who you are without any judgments or trying to change you.

You need to surround yourself with genuine and trustworthy people because having real friendships in your life is very important for many reasons.

The Importance of Having Genuine Friendships

When it comes to friends, it's the quality, not the quantity, that matters. It is better to have three, two, or even one true friend than to have ten unreal ones. Believe it or not, having fake friends will make you unhappy and alone, even if you have dozens of them around you. A bona fide friend will make you feel less alone as they will always be by your side, unlike fake friends who wouldn't care less. They will also listen to you whenever you have a problem and give you helpful advice. Everyone needs a good friend to vent and talk to when they have problems. A true friend will make you feel more confident. They will remind you of how solid you are whenever you doubt yourself. They will cheer you on with all their might as if they were at a Harry Styles concert. A good friend will never get tired of telling you how beautiful, funny, and smart you are, especially when you're feeling down. You may go through harsh times, like losing a pet or your grandparent, and you will need a shoulder to cry on. A good friend will hold you when you cry, listen to you non-stop, and try to find ways to cheer you up. Overall, having a genuine friend in your life will make you happy and less stressed.

How to Find Good Friends

Making friends isn't as hard as you may think. You just need to know where to start.

Be Confident

Approaching new people isn't easy, and it takes grit. However, widening your social circle and making new friends is necessary. You can't know if someone is a good friend or not until you get to know them first. So don't hesitate to approach the new kid in school or talk to mutual friends at a birthday party. Some people can be shy, introverted, or have anxiety, making it difficult for them to go up to someone new and start a conversation. Remember that meeting new people or talking to them isn't that bad; it can actually be lots of fun. It's only your anxiety and nerves that are giving you these thoughts. Once you begin talking, you will realize how exciting it is to get to know someone new, and most people are just as nervous as you about meeting someone new. So, approach them with a smile that will relax your and their nerves and let the conversation flow naturally.

Accept Invitations

Whether it's a birthday party, going away party, a slumber party, or simply to hang out, don't say no to social invitations. These events will provide you with the perfect opportunity to meet new people your age and socialize. If you aren't social, you will find yourself constantly declining invitations. Remember, if you keep saying no to every invitation, your friends and classmates will stop inviting you. Even if you don't feel like it, try to get over it every once in a while, to socialize so you can meet potential friends.

Meet Your Friends' Friends

If you have real and true friends in your life, they will be more than happy to introduce you to their friends. These friends may actually turn out to be genuine people that you can trust and befriend. You may also find things in common between you and them since they are already friends with people you get along with.

Traits to Look For

Now that you know how you can find friends, it's time to discover what to look for in a friend. Remember, you will never know what a person is like right away, so get to know them first, and don't judge them by their mistakes. You should also know that everybody looks for these traits in friends. While looking for them in other people, try to develop them in yourself.

Loyalty

It isn't an exaggeration to say that loyalty should be the main quality you seek in a friend. Look for a friend who will drop everything when you send a text saying you need them. Whether it's school, your parents, or someone you have a crush on, a loyal friend will share your problems with you as if they are their own. They will not believe anything people say about you and will come to talk to you first before judging anything. One of the things to look out for that can help you determine if someone is loyal or not is how they talk about their other friends. A loyal friend will never badmouth their friends to you, even when they are mad at them.

Empathy

As mentioned, empathy is a great social skill and a wonderful trait to look for in a friend. An empathetic friend will never judge you because they can feel and understand what you are going through.

Non-Judgmental

A good friend will never judge the choices or the decisions you make. And because of this, you'll not think twice about going to them when you make a mistake or get into trouble. They will never blame you or make you feel bad about yourself.

You Feel Good Around Them

Stay away from people that make you feel worse after spending time with them. Choose friends who have a positive attitude. Everyone can have a bad day or more every now and then; this is normal. However, in general, positive people are upbeat and always make you feel better when you are around them. When you are down, they know how to lift your spirits.

Good Listeners

Another social skill to look for in a friend is listening skills. They will listen to you when you have a problem, be attentive when you share a story with them, and ask questions to be engaged in the conversation.

Dependable

A good friend is someone you can depend on. They keep their word, are there when you need them, and always have your back. That said, there will be moments when they may fail to be there for you, and that's ok. Your friend isn't Superman, who can do many things at once. There will be moments when their life or school will get in the way. However, you generally know they are people you can depend on because they rarely ever break a promise.

Supportive

Life would be really hard without supportive friends. Support can come in different ways, like supporting your decisions and respecting your choices. Good friends support you emotionally, especially when feeling down or doubting yourself. They will always encourage you to carry on trying. Everyone needs a supportive friend in their lives.

Similar Interests

Your interests and hobbies are much more fun when you do them with others. Whether you love to read, play sports, or play video games, find friends who share the same interests as you, so you will have things to talk about and do together. You should also befriend people with whom you share similar traits, like having the same sense of humor. This will help you establish a bond together.

Using Charm and Humor to Make Friends

Here's a secret - charm and a sense of humor will take you far in life and will help you make new friends. People are always around those who make them laugh. You have it in you to charm people and use your sense of humor to make new friends and keep current ones.

Learn to Take a Joke

Yes, you are growing up, but this doesn't mean you should take yourself seriously. It's ok to laugh at a joke at your expense as long as it isn't ill-intentioned. Friends like to make fun of each other, these jokes are usually harmless. When you laugh at yourself, instead of being offended or turning the whole situation into a drama, this will show others that you have a sense of humor.

For instance - you're walking to class with your best friend and one of their friends, and you have your headphones on and begin to sing loudly. Your best friend tells you, "Hey, Beyonce, you're throwing a free concert for the entire school," they shout and then burst out laughing. This is clearly a harmless joke, so instead of getting upset, laugh at yourself. You can even join in on the joke and say, "well, queen B got nothing on me." This will show your best friend's friend that you not only have a sense of humor but can laugh at yourself and take a joke.

Smile

One of the main characteristics of charming people is that they always meet you with a smile. Whenever you meet someone for the first time, make sure to greet them with a smile. This will make you seem warm and approachable. Just make sure that your smile is genuine. For instance, one of your friends invites you to your birthday party. They also invited all their friends from their old school. When you arrive, they make sure to introduce you to everyone. Smile while you greet these people. You may make a couple of friends by the end of this party.

Make Jokes about Yourself

Humor is a great tool to use when meeting people for the first time. Find ways to make jokes about yourself without appearing desperate or insulting yourself. You can use sarcasm or wit to show that you are both smart and funny. For instance, you are hanging out with a group of people, and you are discussing your grades. You have recently flunked a test that you feel kind of embarrassed about. Instead of saying, "I flunked a test, and I feel horrible," say something like, "well, I recently failed a science test, and I'm sure Isaac Newton is turning over in his grave right now." Making jokes at your expense is similar to taking jokes about you; they show people that you are lighthearted and confident enough to laugh at yourself.

Avoid Making Jokes at Others' Expenses

It's ok to joke about your friends, provided you know they don't mind and that the jokes are well-intentioned. However, avoid making jokes at others' expense if you have just met them or have only recently known them. Don't chime in even if their friends are making fun of them. People will see you as a polite and caring person, which makes them want to get to know you better. Keep the sarcasm and jokes to the friends you have known for a while.

Accept Compliments

Compliments are always nice, and they usually make people good about themselves. However, some people struggle with accepting compliments. They either feel awkward or lack the self-esteem to believe they deserve it. Sometimes, when you meet people for the first time, they may compliment you. Learn to accept compliments by being confident and believing that you deserve them. People complement each other to make them feel good about themselves. Use your charm to return the favor. For instance, your best friend is introducing you to their cousin, and one of them tells you, "Wow, I love your shirt. It looks so cool." Give them a big warm smile, and say, "Thank you so much; I love your shirt too, nice color." This is one way for the cousin and you to make a great first impression on one another.

How to Handle Various Situations

In your day-to-day life, you will be in many situations where you will need to talk to people. These are a few examples of common situations and how to handle them.

New Kid at School

A new kid has just joined your school. Understand that they must feel shy, overwhelmed, and anxious since this is the first day in a new place with new people. They are nervous, and they don't know what to expect. When a kid joins your school, be the first person to make them feel welcome. Smile at them, say hello, and introduce yourself. Ask them to sit with you at lunch and introduce them to your friends. However, if you don't have friends at school, then sit with them at lunch and get to know each other. Follow them on Instagram, TikTok, and other social media platforms. Invite them to groups that will make them feel included. Give them tips on handling different situations in school and help familiarize them with various school activities. You could be making a friend for life.

Your First Crush

Do you think a girl in your class is funny? Do you find the new boy in school cute? Do you blush wherever a specific classmate talks to you? Congratulations! You have your first crush. If they like you, you will know. However, there are certain things that you can do to get their attention. Don't look away whenever you make eye contact with them in class or in the hallway. Look them in the eyes for a couple of seconds and smile the look away. Dress in nice clothes that make you feel confident. Try to figure out their interests by checking their social media pages or watching them. Make sure they see you listening, talking about their favorite band, or reading their favorite book. They may come over to you and start talking to you about the things you are both interested in. If you become friends, get to know them better by asking them questions and showing interest in their lives. Listen to them and make sure to remember details about them. Invite them to a party or a social gathering so you will have the chance to meet in a more relaxed and casual setting other than the school. Whenever you talk, make sure to make eye contact, smile, and use your sense of humor whenever appropriate.

What to Do When You Are Stranded

You may find yourself stranded and lost in a strange place, like when you are camping or on a school trip with no cell phone coverage. The first thing to do is to stay calm. You will not be able to think clearly if you freak out. Stay where you are. Chances are, adults are looking for you, so it is better to remain in your place. However, if where you feel weird and unsafe, move to the nearest safe area. Try to find any adults around you; your teachers or supervisors may be closer than you think. If there is no one nearby, call out their names out loud. If no one hears you, ask anyone nearby for help. However, be smart and don't go anywhere with them. Make sure to only approach people who seem decent and okay.

Making friends isn't hard; you just need to let go of the nerves and have the guts to put yourself out there. Real and genuine friendships are important as they will make you feel supported, less alone, and happy. At the end of the day, remember one thing: the quality, not the quantity, that counts.

Chapter 6: The Road to Independence

Being independent is a very important quality to learn when you are a tween. In this chapter, you'll understand what it is and how it can help you grow and develop into a better person. You'll also understand how to make the right decisions, so you can rely less on those around you.

What Does It Mean to Be Independent?

Many people think that to be independent, you must prove yourself every step of the way. They think that independence is earned when you can prove that you are better than everyone else in everything. However, this is not true. Being independent doesn't mean you need to get the highest grades in your class, be the best player on your team, have the largest number of friends, and do all your chores perfectly simultaneously. We all have weaknesses, but this doesn't make us dependent on others.

Being independent simply means that you know your strengths and weaknesses. For instance, you are an independent student if you realize that you're great at literature, but math isn't your strongest course, so you decide to spend more time on it. Independent people don't wait for anyone to come along to offer a helping hand. Instead of waiting for one of your parents to help you out or tell you what to do, you grow some and become better. Being independent means asking your teachers for help with the courses you are not so good at. Independent athletes know their strongest suit and what they need to work on. For example, if they know they're fast runners but have weak upper body muscles, they will go to the gym to work on that.

In other words, being independent means you don't need anyone to tell you to do this or do that. You are already always working on becoming a better version of yourself. Independent people have a lot of self-belief. They believe that they will succeed no matter how tough the situation is. They are also at peace with themselves. This means that they know that they're putting in the effort, regardless of the results. Even the best football players don't win every game they play.

Independent people are also caring, compassionate, and considerate. They should be able to care for themselves and those around them without waiting for anything in return. For some people, this is one of the hardest things to do. This is because when we try to be nice to someone, it's only natural to expect something in return. So, the independent thing to do is to get rid of this expectation so you won't need anyone to make you feel happy, loved, strong, or fulfilled.

People come and go all the time. Even when no one else is there for you, being independent means that you'll always be there for yourself. Your strength and independence are something that no one can ever take away from you. Independent individuals seldom feel insecure because they are at peace with their insecurities.

Are People Who Need Help Dependent?

Many people make the mistake of thinking that kids who need help are weak and dependent on others. We all need help sometimes, which never takes away from our independence. Dependent people are those who are unwilling to put in the effort to change. The difference between independent and dependent kids is that independent people ask for help when they need to because they want to become better people, and dependent individuals, on the other hand, ask for help because they want to take the easy way out.

Let's return to our student example. While independent students recognize their weak points, go to their teacher for help, and then study everything they learn, the dependent student may not even try to figure out what they don't understand. Instead, they may ask their parents for help and expect to be spoon-fed the information. Some dependent students copy their friends' assignments without even trying to do the work themselves. They know that they're not good at math, so instead of trying to turn the situation around, they'll just tell themselves, "I will never get it even if I try." What's the point?

Part of being independent is knowing when to ask for help without abusing the helping hand. We all need others to help us out at times so we can move forward in life. People who believe they can do everything independently and refuse to accept help from others are also unlikely to succeed. No one can do everything perfectly. We each have unique passions, interests, hobbies, and talents, which is why we need one another. Talking to others about your weaknesses and asking for help is not a sign of dependence. It comes from a place of great strength and security.

Seeking help shows just how dedicated, ambitious, and hard-working you are. As weird as it sounds, being unafraid to ask for help can signify confidence. Only insecure individuals are afraid to admit when there's something that they don't know or can't do. They worry that it might make other people think less of them. However, if you are confident and secure about yourself and your abilities, you'll know that your value isn't based on how much or how little you can do. If your friends think less of you because you can't juggle being an A+ student and an athlete, then they aren't your friends. There is no shame in saying, "I don't know." Other kids will see someone who is honest and confident if you can say this and ask for help.

There is nothing better than thanking the people who gave you a helping hand along the way. It makes you appear as much more than just strong or dedicated. It makes you a kind and appreciative person who never takes advantage of others. The worst people are those who take all the credit for themselves and totally disregard the people who helped them get where they are.

Independence

The concept of independence can be quite confusing. You're probably wondering, "How can I ask for help and not have people think I need to rely on others?" or "When should I start this whole independence thing?" or "okay, but what does independence really mean?"

Independence grows naturally whenever you enter your teenage years because this is when you rely on your parents less. You may get a job and start making money. So instead of asking your parents to pay for everything you need, you'll be able to pitch in, giving you more independence. If you juggle different schedules or eat a different diet than your parents, you may start cooking your own meals. The older you grow, the more independent you'll become. It's a major step in transitioning from being a teenager to an adult.

The earlier you practice independence, the easier it will become when you grow up. Technically, you can't move out or get a job right now, but there are many ways to practice independence at your age. If your parents still help you study or revise for your exams, you should try to do that yourself. The results may not be that good. However, you will know that this is your own effort. In time, you will figure out the best study technique for you and watch your grades rise once again. You may offer to do your own laundry if you're not already doing it. The first few laundry batches may not be perfect, but that's okay.

There isn't a single age when everyone becomes fully independent because no one is truly entirely independent. We all need help sometimes, which is fine. You should never compare your own efforts to others because we all go through life at our own pace. Just because your friend prepares her lunch bag doesn't mean you need to. We all have different responsibilities and priorities in life. As long as you're doing your part, this is all that matters.

The Importance of Independence

Sometimes, trying to be too independent can be a bad thing. Besides, ending up feeling isolated because you have gone over the top with insisting on doing everything on your own, even if you don't know how it can result in failure. However, learning how to rely on yourself at an early age is a life lesson that everyone needs to learn, especially in the fast-paced world in which we live. Not only does it prepare you for adulthood, but it would also benefit you in many other areas of your life.

Serves as a Self-Confidence and Self-Esteem Booster

Being independent gives you the trust that you need in your capabilities. It makes you feel confident that you're skilled enough to handle anything that comes your way. This self-assurance serves as a self-esteem booster. It also gives you a more positive outlook on life.

Reduces Stress and Makes You Happier

Being emotionally independent will mean you can manage your feelings more effectively. This makes you a better problem-solver, which promotes confidence. Your stress levels are reduced when you no longer need to wait for someone to come to your rescue whenever you have a problem. Some moments in life are already stressful as they come. Waiting for people to help you out and weigh in on their opinion can only add to the pressure. You can regain control over your life by dealing with those situations alone. You can handle your stress more effectively by focusing only on what you can control.

Leads to Better Decision-Making

We make a thousand different decisions each day. From choosing what to eat for breakfast to determining which homework assignment to start with, many of these decisions go unnoticed. While some choices are wider than others, we often need to take the time to look at the evidence and facts and weigh the pros and cons of each choice before we settle on a decision. Unfortunately, decision-making can stress many people out, making the wrong choices. For instance, if you don't want to think about what to pack for lunch, you can just grab a bag of chips instead of making a healthy sandwich and slicing up an apple. A lack of independence can also cause you to pass up on your own happiness. This is because you end up doing what everyone else wants without considering your own wants and needs first.

It Enables You to Be of Assistance
Have you ever heard the phrase "you can't pour from an empty cup"? How can you help other people if you have nothing to give them? If you rely on others for physical, emotional, or school support, then you won't be able to help anyone else with that stuff. Being independent means that you can help out. This can make you feel a lot happier and more supported. When we're useful to others, we get to feel a sense of purpose. We also feel generally happier in life.

Promotes Inner Peace
Many people get confused between independence and selfishness. However, they are not the same. Independent people are very aware of their wants and needs. They know what to do to make themselves happy and fulfilled. Independent individuals seldom stress over things they have no control over, which is why they have a sense of inner peace. Selfish people only think of themselves and how they can get things from other people for themselves.

Allows You to Prioritize Your Needs
Independent individuals know how to put themselves first, which is never bad. You need to care for yourself and make sure that all your needs are met so that you don't burn out. Stress can be very bad for your mental, emotional, and physical health.

Helps You Focus on Your Goals
Learning to be independent can open up endless opportunities for you. It helps you focus on your goals and gives you a much broader and more pos-

itive way of thinking. Instead of dwelling on all the reasons why something won't work out, you start thinking about how it can work out. Practicing independence takes you to new places and helps you meet new people. When you don't rely on others, you end up going on new adventures, and without knowing it, you will be leaning into your creative side for help. Since being independent makes you a better decision-maker, it helps with feeling more peaceful, improves self-confidence, and reduces stress; you can focus more of your time and effort on your goals. This is how you grow and develop. It helps you challenge yourself to get out of your comfort zone.

How to Make Better Decisions

Decision-making can sometimes make you feel worried because you are scared of making the wrong one or haven't worked out what you think will be the best way for you to go. This is when you need to ensure you have all the facts about the issue to make a smart decision. To make this much easier, it helps to have a process that you can follow. This process works for every decision that you need to make:

1. **Extend the Deadline**
   You can't make a good decision if you are under pressure to do it quickly. It is a surefire way to select the wrong choice. It doesn't matter if you work well under pressure. Taking a few minutes to determine your choices and then consider the facts can help you make the right choice. Take a mental note of the pros and cons of each possible decision. If possible, try to sleep on it to see if your opinion changes in the morning. There will come moments in life, whether at school or later on at work, when you will need to be quick to decide. Always ask for extra time to think if you need it.

2. **Make Sure You Have All the Facts**

   Do you need to assign roles in your group project? Are you worried that you'll end up having to do all the work in the end? In situations like this, you must ensure you have all the facts before making any decisions. For instance, ask your friends what they do best and consider their strengths, weaknesses, favorite subjects, interests, and skills before you hand out the tasks. If one of your friends is creative, they can handle that side of the presentation or project. If someone enjoys researching and looking things up, they can be responsible for figuring out the history of your topic. If you're the group leader, your teacher probably assigned you that role because she thinks you have good organizational skills. Use facts and evidence along with your own judgment to make good decisions.

3. **Consider the Consequences**

   Consider the consequences of your decision. Will your friends disagree with you? If you're worried this may happen, let them add their bit to the decision-making process. Tell them why you think each person would be fit for the chosen role and see if they agree with you.

4. **Ask for Input**

   Be open to other people's opinions and see if their advice works for you. It also helps to ask for the input of someone who is removed from the situation. For example, you may want to ask your teacher for help. Explain that you think that your friend should handle the historical aspect of the project because she's a great researcher, but she believes she would be a better fit for executing the experiment. Listen to what your teacher has to say and make a decision you feel confident about.

5. **Be Flexible**

   While this is a simple and easy process that you can use in most situations, you will have to improvise at times. You will often need to take different steps to handle the situation, so be ready to adopt a flexible approach.

You already do many things that you may not realize are signs of independence. Walking home from school, organizing your room, picking out your clothes, putting away your laundry, feeding your dog, and washing your dishes are all examples of being independent. Don't worry about how independent you are because chances are that you're more independent than you believe you are. You're good to go as long as you don't rely on others to do things for you just because you don't want to do them.

Chapter 7: Using Technology

In this day and age, we use technology as often as we eat or sleep. Our smartphones have become our whole world. And we can find out anything we want to at the touch of a screen., providing us with numerous resources just with a touch of our hands. However, technology has also brought with it several disadvantages, especially for pre-teens and teens. Children and pre-adolescents are by far the most affected by the use of technology. While it may provide entertainment for hours and even contains unlimited educational resources, some harmful effects need to be avoided no matter what.

Children around the age of 11- 12 are often the most vulnerable to the dangers of the internet, social media, and in general, technology. This is the time when you get exposed to various technological devices and are allowed to join different social media platforms. And while these social media platforms promise they have high safety guidelines, they are not always completely safe. Therefore, you need to understand the risks that come with the use of technology as well as social media.

On the other hand, many educational resources can help your education and will be excellent for your personality development. So, while there's no argument that technology and social media are essential for everyone these days, proper precautions should be taken, and safety measures should be set to ensure your safety.

Why Too Much Screen Time Is Detrimental

When you're talking about screen time, don't just consider the time you spend using your phone. Remember, other technological devices you use daily contribute to your daily average screen time. These can include your laptop, PC, TV, video games, projectors, iPads, or Tablets. It is a lot when you combine the screen time of all of these devices, even when you're using them subconsciously. Excessive screen time can lead to several health issues, not just physical but also mental. The harmful rays emitted from the use of these devices are the main culprit behind these detrimental effects. Some of these include:

1. **Behavioral Issues**
   Screen time can become an addiction really quickly. Research has linked excessive screen time with behavioral problems in children and teenagers. If you spend too much time on a screen, you could have problems staying attentive and often be cranky or frustrated. Too much exposure to screens can make you mentally fatigued, which results in an automatic feeling of frustration and annoyance. Although it is hard to connect the use of devices with frustrated and annoying behavior, many signs point toward it. If you still don't believe it, try to notice how you behave the next time you spend a few hours playing video games or binge-watching a show.

2. **Risk of Obesity**
   The more you use devices to watch movies, shows, videos, or play video games, the more likely you are to be at risk of being overweight and even obese. Many children develop an appetite for junk food and an excessive amount of food from online ads. Plus, the more you sit in one place and look at your screen, whether you're eating or not, the more unhealthy your lifestyle will be. Even if you're not obese or

near it, just imagine where your habits will lead. Most teens eat while watching movies or shows, even if they're not hungry. This can lead to an unhealthy amount of weight being gained.

3. **Poor Academic Performance**
   If you are exposed to too many electronic devices and screens, you will most likely show poor academic performance than people who aren't. Thus, academic performance can be directly linked with how much screen time you use and how you manage it. When you have all your interest in video games or movies, you're more likely not to pay attention to any of the stuff being discussed in class. This obvs means your grades will suffer, even in your favorite subjects.

4. **Disturbance in Sleep**
   Did you know that sleep problems are caused by excessive screen time? Many people believe that watching television before bed will make them fall asleep faster; however, this is not true - any kind of screen exposure before bed can result in an irregular sleeping pattern. The excessive use of devices before bed can even lead to insomnia. This is mainly due to the blue light emitted from screens that mess with your sleep patterns.

5. **Violent Behavior**
   If you watch too much violence on your screens, you'll become desensitized to it and what it means, and some people even start believing that it's a normal way to solve problems. A load of movies, video games, shows, and other online platforms show violent content, which can have to scar your mind. Because you are at the age when all sorts of things are developing, you need to be especially careful not to copy any violent behavior you see being promoted through games and movies.

Use of Social Media, Why or Why Not?

Social media use is normal if you have access to the internet; however, because there are so many weirdos and dodgy things that can happen, you need to be clever about the time you spend online to stay safe. Every day, new and innovative social media platforms are being developed, each for a different purpose. While using these platforms brings many good things for you, they can also be unsafe and damaging if you're not careful. Therefore, it's important to find a balance when using these sites. There are arguments of both kinds about this topic; while some adults want to limit their children's use of social media for many reasons, others want them to have access to many other benefits that the use of social media entails. So, here's a list of why you should or shouldn't use social media as a pre-teen.

1. **Helps Learn Skills**

    While there's so much hate regarding social media being toxic and unhealthy for you, it actually has some cool, strong points that are at odds with this argument. Social media's significant resource in a teenager's life is indisputable. To grow and develop an impressive personality, you need to have skills in your court that make you distinguishable from the rest of the crowd. Many social media accounts have been designed especially for the career and personality development of pre-adolescent kids. Before social media, learning skills were a lot harder to get than they are today.

2. **Loneliness Factor**

    One of the many disadvantages of the frequent use of social media among kids and teens is the loneliness factor. While you'd think social media was designed to get people closer together, to eliminate the boundaries of the physical world, and although it does help connect people together, it is also the reason people don't meet up as often. You might feel extra lonely when you see other people's stories and feel totally left out and jealous. And you could feel disconnected from the world, even when you're technically connected through social media. As compared to the days before the internet, and social media, friend get-togethers also don't happen that often anymore.

3. **Helps with Money Management**
You'd be surprised to know that social media can be a great resource for earning money, not just for adults but for teenagers. You can create innovative products and sell them on social media platforms. Many pages can teach a lot about sales, advertisement, marketing, and other business skills. You can also work towards being a social media influencer and earn money doing stuff you love. This way, you will not only earn some money on the side but also learn how to manage your money effectively.

4. **Promotes Materialism**
The whole purpose of social media is to share your activities, likes, dislikes, and basically everything about your life. While no one forces you to post your personal information on social media, teenagers tend to overshare their personal information. Often, they share this information on public accounts, meaning everyone in the world can get access to their information. Keep in mind that you are at the age where you're in the process of trying to figure out your personality, and at this ripe age, any comments or remarks can hurt if you're not careful. Social media can promote materialism if you start considering it to be definitive of your worth. For instance, if you do not get enough likes or comments on your pictures or posts, you may start doubting yourself and let this measure your self-worth.

5. **Enhances Creativity**
Social media is full of creative stuff by people from all over the world. In a time when you are still exploring your personality, polishing your skills, and trying to find interests, social media can be your guiding

light. Many people share their ideas, art, music, and other creative works on social media. This can help you learn and change things up to come up with unique ideas of your own.

6. **Attracts Unwanted Attention**
   Social media brings you unwanted attention, and while it is easier for adults to handle unwanted attention and criticism, the same is not true for young people. Social media can bring out the worst in some people, and they would love nothing but to bring others down with them. Whether it's hateful comments, cyberbullying, inappropriate messages, or any other form of social media hate, you need someone to help you handle it if it happens to you.

Smart Usage of Technology

The use of technology is, unfortunately, something that cannot be eliminated completely. Although there are many negative effects of using technology, it also comes with so many benefits. So, you need to manage your screen time instead of trying to stop it completely and failing.

Understandably, you need to use technology for your school and some recreational activities, but that doesn't mean there should be no limits to your usage. To be a smart, growing individual, you must start changing your screen habits and developing a smart screen schedule. Here are some ways to limit your screen time without restricting your study time.

1. **Track Screen Time and Set Limits**
   So, while you probably think you don't have excessive screen time, that might not be true. To get out of your ignorance is bliss mentality, the best thing you can do is track your screen time to get an idea of how

much of that glorious blue light you're exposing yourself to. There are lots of off-screen time-tracking apps available for both your desktop and phone. The best part about these apps? They will track the time you've spent using each app and also the total for your day.

Moreover, you can also set time limits on these apps. For instance, if you've set a limit on your Instagram usage for 30 minutes a day, the screen time tracking app will not allow you to access Instagram for the rest of the day. Similarly, you can do this for every app and streaming platform to control your average screen time.

2. **Keep Your Phone and Television Out of the Bedroom**
Almost everyone today has made it their bedtime ritual to use their phone before sleep and as soon as they wake up. This habit is, in fact, extremely damaging to not just your sleep schedule but also your eyesight. Plus, using your phone right before bed is always bad because you end up staying up later than you'd planned. This, in turn, ruins your ability to wake up on time the next day. The only solution to these bad habits is to keep your phone in another room when you go to sleep. If you use it as an alarm clock, it might be time to substitute it with a real alarm clock. The same goes for your television. If a TV is installed in your room, it will keep you up and distracted from sleep. It is, therefore, better to have TVs installed in the living room rather than in your bedroom.

3. **Establish Tech-Free Zones**
A good way to minimize screen time is to establish tech-free zones where you don't use any technology. For instance, you can add bathrooms to this list; using your phone there is not just unsanitary but also makes you waste your time, and if it gets wet, it is costly to replace. The dining room should also be a no-tech zone. Although many people have a habit of eating while watching movies or videos, this habit takes away precious time you could spend with your family.

4. **Uninstall Unnecessary Apps**

   Make a thorough sweep of your phone and remove any apps that may seem useless or become a distraction when you're working. For instance, you can remove social media sites you only use for school and access them through your computer. You should also remove streaming apps from your phone as they tend to distract you from work.

5. **Pick up a New Hobby**

   The best way to reduce your screen time is to pick up a new hobby. Hobbies bring out your creative side and also help your personality development. You'll notice that you turn to your phone, TV, or laptop when you're bored instead of doing something else. Unfortunately, this is what a lot of us are guilty of doing. So, to reduce your screen time, pick up a new hobby. It doesn't matter if it's art, cooking, or reading, as long as it's off-screen.

Smart Social Networking

Social media is a great resource and something you should stay wary of. So, it's important to stay vigilant while you use different social media platforms for socializing, networking, and learning. Here are some ways you can practice smart social networking as a pre-teen.

1. **Don't Post Anything Inappropriate**

   Try not to post anything inappropriate on your social media profile. You never know where you'll be tomorrow or any other day, and to ensure a good future, you should have a good online presence. Think of the impression your family, future employers, or college admission people would get. Before making any rash, or inappropriate posts, consider if you would be okay with your statement or picture being attached to you for the rest of your life.

2. **Build a Positive Online Reputation**

   Creating a positive online presence doesn't just start when you're prepping for college admissions. You need to have a positive presence on social media by actively participating in social campaigns, volunteering activities, academic competitions, etc. You could write blogs or articles for online pages and news outlets to make an impressive online presence. All of these activities will look pretty remarkable on your CV. There are many ways you can create a good online presence.

3. **Don't Compromise Your Identity**

   Identity theft is a common online crime, and most criminals target kids or elderly folk. If these people get your personal information from online sources, they will try to make money at your expense. So, make sure never to post your date of birth, address, phone number, social security number, or any other private information online. Although some platforms do require your date of birth and contact, you should never trust unreliable sources and apps.

4. **Be Considerate of Others**

   If someone doesn't respond to your message, instead of harassing them, you should take the hint and move on. Moreover, you must know how serious it is to post someone's picture online without their permission. If someone asks you to remove their picture, post, or untag them, you should do so without question.

5. **Don't Share Your Location**

   You wouldn't want to give a stranger your daily agenda, so why do it through social media? Many burglaries and abductions occur after the criminal has stalked the victim's social media profile to get familiar with their schedule and location. So, keep your whereabouts private and not accessible to everyone on social media.

The use of technology is an inevitable part of our lives, and while we should be used to this, we should never let it reach excessive levels. Excessive use of anything is not healthy, and the same goes for technology, the internet, and social media. You need to be smart when using all of these things because they won't always bring you benefits and may sometimes lead to serious problems.

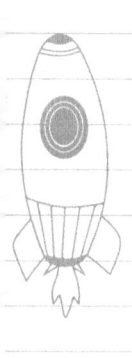

Chapter 8 — Managing Body Changes

Being a pre-teen can be an awkward time for anyone. You're growing up faster than ever before, and there is pressure from social media, school, and friends, and you have more responsibility than ever. And all of these changes can be a lot to deal with. With this in mind, you need to know a number of things about how the body changes too.

This chapter will discuss how growing up is normal but challenging for most tweens. As you get older, you start developing physically as well as mentally. At this stage of your life, you become less childlike and start maturing and becoming more independent at the same time.

So, What Happens?

Worrying about your body undergoing changes as you grow is normal. But remember that these changes happen to everyone. Before puberty starts, you'll probably experience a growth spurt. Girls experience this between the ages of 8 and 13, and boys between the ages of 10 and 15. There is even a possibility that you will grow between 3 and 4 inches (9 to 10 centimeters) per year!

When the first signs of puberty show up, you can expect to develop body odor and start growing hair in new places too. You might also have mood swings, as well as trouble concentrating. And to put the cherry on top, you could notice that you don't have as much energy as you used to. But there's nothing to worry about. These are all signs that you're growing up.

You'll likely experience several physical changes. Some of these include:

- An increase in height, weight, and muscle mass - Girls grow faster than boys, but boys gain more muscle mass and end up heavier.
- An increase in body fat is normal and necessary for growth.
- Changes in body shape - Girls and boys start developing curves and will likely become more self-conscious about their weight.
- New hair growth - Girls will get hair on their legs, armpits, and pubic hair. Boys will grow pubic, armpit, and facial hair.

When these changes begin, don't think you are alone - everyone is simultaneously going through the same things. In cases where you feel self-conscious, it's not uncommon for you to start noticing things about your appearance and begin to wonder if something is wrong (there really isn't anything wrong). You should avoid comparing yourself to your peers because you'll just be making yourself stressed for nothing; everyone around your age feels the same.

Welcome to Puberty!

Puberty is the time in your life when your body begins to change from a child into an adult. It's normal for you and everyone else around you to go through this change at some point. Puberty happens when hormones in your body begin to spike, causing your body to grow and develop. These changes don't just happen overnight. Puberty is an ongoing process that starts around age 8 and finishes by the time you reach 15 years of age. Some people might go through it earlier or later than others, but it's not something you can control. The good news is that almost all of these changes are completely natural and healthy, so you don't have anything to worry about.

Knowing What to Expect Can Help

Nobody likes surprises, and puberty is full of them. Many changes are happening to your body, and knowing what to expect and when to plan ways to cope with them can be helpful. For example, your first period is something every girl prepares for. Your first shaving experience will be less surprising if you know that the hair on your legs will likely become thicker and darker. And your first pimple- or 10- is less embarrassing if you know how the hormones in your body are causing it to happen. One of the best things about puberty is that it's a one-time thing that happens to everyone.

Physical Changes Happen Because of Hormones

Hormones are chemicals that are produced inside your body. They travel through your blood and relay messages between different body parts. As you grow up, your body begins to produce more hormones, which is one of the main reasons your body and mind change at this time. Hormones are responsible for many functions in your body, including regulating your growth, controlling your metabolism, and enabling you to have children. Hormones are powerful substances that greatly impact your health and well-being. They're also pretty finicky, so it's important to look after them. You can reduce the stress hormones put on your body by getting plenty of rest, eating a healthy diet, and avoiding anything bad for you.

Why Do Our Bodies Change During Puberty?

Puberty is a process that is triggered when the pituitary gland releases a substance called gonadotropin. This hormone travels through your bloodstream, which is responsible for all the changes that occur during puberty. The hormones produced during puberty are primarily estrogen and testosterone.

- Estrogen is responsible for the changes in your breasts and reproductive organs. It increases your bust size and can cause your periods to become more frequent and heavier. Estrogen also stimulates your clitoris, urethra, and labia to grow.

- Testosterone is responsible for many of the physical changes that occur in boys. It causes your voice to deepen, your muscles to grow, and your body hair to grow thicker. Testosterone also stimulates the production of sperm cells.

Changes in Boys During Puberty

The changes in boys' bodies during puberty are very noticeable. Some of the most noticeable changes are the growth of hair and voice changes. These changes usually start in the early stages of puberty and can take years to complete. At the time of puberty, most boys will have a growth spurt of over an inch per year. During this time, boys will grow taller and gain more muscle mass. They will also develop more skin oil and sweat glands. Puberty begins with the increase in testicle size, the contraction of the scrotum, and the development of bumps on the scrotum. As puberty progresses, the penis begins to develop and mature as well. After the onset of changes in the scrotum, pubic hair grows quickly but may initially appear thin due to the changes in the scrotum. During puberty, most boys will have an increase in their libido or sex drive. This can result in erections during sleep or when they are not aroused. Boys also grow hair in their armpits, legs, and pubic region.

Changes in Girls During Puberty

Girls go through puberty at different stages and different ages, but the changes are similar to those in boys. Girls will grow more body hair and have changes in their menstrual cycle. They will also grow taller and develop more muscle and body fat, but they do not have as much growth spurt as boys. During puberty, girls' breasts will grow larger, and they experience their first period. Breast size varies widely and isn't usually indicative of breast health. Periods are a sign that a girl has gone through puberty. Girls bleed from the uterus during periods, but they don't always have cramps. A menstrual cycle is the cycle of changes that occur in your uterus and ovaries every month. The process begins when an egg is released from an ovary - this is called ovulation. This is the only day in the menstrual cycle when the chance of becoming pregnant is highest.

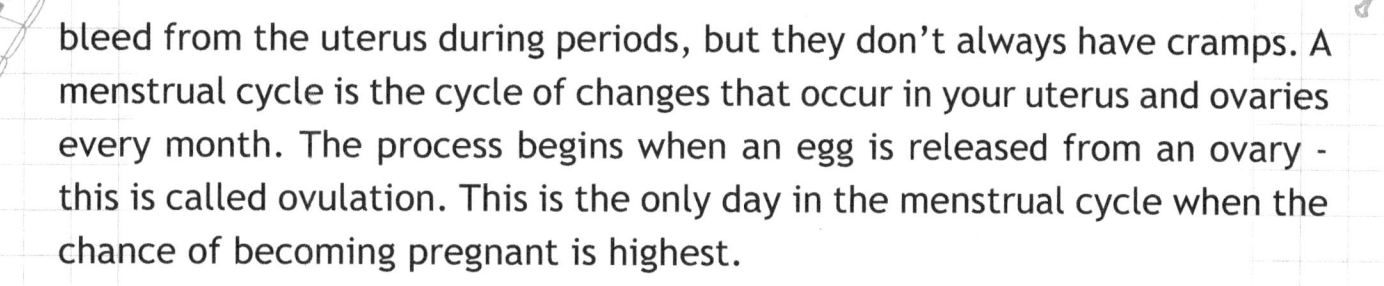

Body Hair

Body hair is another sign of puberty. You'll probably notice hair growing in your armpits, lower legs, and pubic area. The hair growth on your legs and armpits is usually light and fine, while pubic hair tends to be thicker.

Pubic hair helps protect the skin in your pubic area by trapping dirt and bacteria.

Body Shape

Many people experience changes in their body shape during this time. Girls may notice that their hips get wider and their waists get narrower, while boys may notice their shoulders get broader.

Other Things Will Change Too

While boys and girls are growing more muscles and reaching more adult heights, other parts of their bodies will also mature. The brain grows larger and will be more developed. This helps you grow better at making judgments and decisions, and you become more mature. The digestive tract will develop more fully, so you can digest food more easily. The lungs and heart will also grow larger and become stronger. This means you'll be more active without tiring as quickly and will make it easier to breathe.

When Does Puberty Start and End?

The process of puberty can be broken down into two phases: the initial and secondary phases. The initial phase of the process is marked by the emergence of sex hormones and the start of physical and biological changes. The second phase of this process is the continuation and completion of these physical and biological changes.

- **Initial Phase** - The initial phase of puberty usually starts around 10 years of age. However, it can begin as early as 8 years of age or as late as 15 years of age. This phase usually finishes when a person reaches 16 years of age.
- **Secondary Phase** - The secondary phase of puberty starts when the initial phase ends. The majority of physical and biological changes are complete when a person reaches 15 years of age.

Bottom Line

Puberty is the process that changes a child into an adult. It is a complex biological and social process that occurs in all human beings with both female and male sex organs. During puberty, the body experiences many changes. These changes are caused by hormones released from cells in the body. These hormones cause physical changes in the body, such as the growth of body hair, breast development in girls, and the growth of testicles and the growth of the penis in boys. They also cause emotional changes such as mood swings, increased libido, and anxiety.

A Final Word: Don't Be Discouraged

Puberty can be overwhelming with all of the big changes that are happening in your body. It may seem like your body is completely out of control and doing strange things that aren't normal. Remember that it will pass if you feel like puberty is too much to handle. These changes will become less frequent and intense as you get older and will one day end completely. There are also ways you can cope with the more uncomfortable symptoms. For example, you can minimize acne breakouts with a skincare routine, make sure your bowels are moving regularly with fiber supplements, and treat cramps with heat packs. And you can also look forward to the positive changes that puberty brings. Puberty is the beginning of your blossoming into an adult and all of the exciting things that come with it.

5 Ways to Cope with Puberty and Your Changing Body

With all the changes happening, you will feel really weird sometimes. You may feel confused, frustrated, and anxious about how your body changes and develops. Your new body might also bring you new challenges in your social life. These changes can be scary and confusing – especially if you've never seen them happen. Feeling embarrassed or self-conscious about these changes is natural, but you should know that these experiences are completely normal for teenagers. Understanding what is happening to your body will help you cope with the changes more effectively. Here are 5 ways to cope with puberty and your changing body.

Have a Few Trusted People to Talk To

The changes can leave you feeling embarrassed, confused, or even depressed. Having a few trusted people to talk to about these feelings will help you see things clearly and cope with them better. If you're not comfortable talking to your parents about how you're feeling, you might want to consider finding another adult to who you can talk. You can also think about reaching out to a friend who you trust and feel comfortable confiding in. The people in your life who understand what you're going through can help lift some of the weight off your shoulders. They can also help guide you through any challenges, such as bullying or body image issues.

Exercise and Eat Healthy

As you begin to experience more growth, you might notice that your appetite increases – especially if you are growing faster than expected. So, ensure you're eating a healthy, balanced diet, so your body has the energy it needs. It's also important to make sure you're exercising regularly to keep your body strong, healthy, and fit. If you notice that you're gaining weight, you might want to make changes to your diet to compensate for the increase in your appetite. Avoiding sugary or fatty foods will also help you to avoid growing too quickly. You should also make sure you're drinking enough water to stay hydrated. Exercising regularly will help you stay healthy and fit while also burning any excess calories. Working out can also help relieve the stress many teenagers experience during puberty.

Find Activities You Enjoy

Enjoyable and engaging activities can help you take your mind off your body's changes. They can help you feel less self-conscious about your body and make the most of puberty's experiences. Making the most of your hobbies and interests can also help you to meet new people who can become your friends and support system. These people can help you to stay positive and avoid feeling too self-conscious about your body and what's happening to it. You can choose anything you enjoy and feel comfortable doing. Many teens enjoy common hobbies and interests during puberty, including sports, music, and art.

Get More Sleep

Your body needs more sleep as it grows and develops during puberty. Sleeping each night will help you stay healthy, manage weight, and feel less stressed during puberty. It can also help your body to recover quicker after exercise. Making sure you get enough sleep can be challenging, especially if you're going through other changes that are happening during puberty. These changes can often cause feelings of anxiety and stress. Having a regular sleep schedule and a consistent bedtime can help you with these issues. It can also help you to feel more rested and energized when you get up in the morning.

Learn about Your Body and How to Care for It

Knowing more about your body and what is happening to it can help you feel less confused when you experience these changes. You can learn about the changes your body goes through by reading up on them online or in books. You can also talk to your doctor or other healthcare providers if you have any questions or concerns. Knowing more about what is happening to your body can also help you to make informed decisions about how you care for yourself. You can change your diet and exercise routine to help you stay healthy and fit during puberty. Knowing more about your body and what's happening can also help you feel more confident in your skin. This can help you to feel less self-conscious about your new body and how it's changing.

Bottom Line

Puberty can be a scary and confusing time. But these changes are completely normal. Having a few trusted people to talk with, engaging in enjoyable activities, and getting enough sleep can help to make the most of these experiences.

Kids go through many changes as they grow up and become tweens. This can be an awkward and challenging time. During this time, you'll experience physical and psychological changes. You might become more self-conscious, more aware of social issues, and need more alone time. There are lots of resources available that will help you through these changes and help you feel accepted and understood.

Chapter 9: Channeling Your Emotions

Tween years are one of the trickiest phases for anyone, and to make everything more complicated, you'll also have to deal with emotional complexity. You're already going through countless transitions, and then there are "emotions" that can weigh you down or make you feel the mightiest in a second.

It's, hands down, pretty confusing! Adding to the confusion is all the stress about positive emotions; what or how can you channel and direct your emotions to increase happiness? An interesting fact to be aware of is that negative emotions make their way to our thoughts and behavior faster than positive ones. So, it becomes a tug of war between positive vs. negative emotions, and before you know it, you're in an emotional mess, and you're unable to recall the significance of channeling your emotions.

This chapter will guide you through an overview of why channeling emotions is important and how to do it mindfully. We will also share some benefits of channeling your emotions and a few exercises to help you speed up the process.

Importance of Channeling Your Emotions

Have you ever asked yourself what emotion really is? Well, it is a burst of sentiments, feelings, and sensations, but deep down, it's a chemical reaction happening in your brain. This chemical reaction leads to the experience that we call "emotion."

Unfortunately, we are often encouraged or pressured to suppress and ignore negative emotions. But ignoring these emotions will only make you bottle up your feelings, and you won't be able to get the negative stuff out of your life, or you'll have an emotional explosion. The more you try to suppress your emotions, the more difficult it will get for you, and you'll also be dealing with a lot of anxiety or depression. That's really not a pretty picture and nothing you should deal with in your awesome tween years.

It's hard not to argue that emotions are tricky, whether you focus on the emotions of joy, excitement, love, or frustration, anger, and gloom. It's all messy and complex. However, even with all this messiness, you cannot simply ignore them and their importance.

Our emotions have a long-lasting impact on our mood and everyday life. So, it is not possible to live a healthy life without learning to channel your emotions in a healthy and mindfully positive manner. In this chapter, you'll explore different ways to do just that.

The Art of Mindfulness and Positive Thinking

You may be hearing way too much rant about mindfulness, and it may often sound a bit too much like "adult jargon," doesn't it? Mindfulness and positive thinking are for all ages and have insanely cool benefits you can't miss. Younger kids, tweens, teens, adults, and older people are practicing mindfulness and positive thinking these days. Yes, you heard it...it has become a 'trend.' If that didn't make your heart jump with glee, you have to try the art of mindfulness once to understand its impact.

It helps you channel your emotions and has a very positive influence on your overall mood as well. Before using it, you have to understand what mindfulness and positive thinking are and if there's any difference between the two. Simply put, mindfulness can be described as 'being in the present and staying aware of yourself and your surroundings,' and positive thinking is more about approaching life with a positive and productive perspective.

All of this does not mean that you are ignoring the "negatives" in life; instead, it's more about acknowledging the negative aspects and channeling them towards productivity positively and mindfully.

Positive thinking and mindfulness are close friends because they're linked to giving you more coherence, empathy, and hope. However, these two concepts aren't exactly alike because mindfulness is merely about 'acceptance' and 'being in the present moment'; it doesn't require labeling your thoughts or experiences. Although, this subtle difference doesn't mean we can ignore one or the other idea here because mindfulness helps us use positive thinking to rewrite our past habits and adopt more productive ones.

Benefits of Channeling Your Emotions

You may be wondering if there are any benefits to channeling your emotions at all, or are we just making some hippie statements here? Tween years are already full of excitement, stressors, and so much more that you don't need a new list of things to do unless it's benefiting you somehow!

Channeling your emotions have many benefits, especially for tweens. When you channel your emotions, you can better understand people and their effect on you. So learning how to control your emotions is something you'll have to do, and that's where channeling comes in. Let's review some of the key benefits of channeling your emotions in detail.

1. **Helps to Manage Stress**
   When you are stressed out, you will face more problems with your emotions. This happens especially when you constantly watch out and worry that things might take a stressful turn. It's hard for you to feel happy and content, and your emotions can easily become messy and chaotic.
   If you don't manage your stress well, you could end up with anxiety, depression, and insomnia. This can lead to poor performance at school, work, and home. When you can channel your emotions efficiently and understand how to express them healthily, you are more likely to better deal with stress. It also helps to build self-esteem, which makes you believe you are good enough and deserve respect.

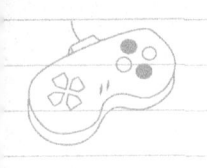

Channeling your emotions will make you more focused and happier by reducing stress significantly. It also helps you to avoid negative consequences that can disturb your mental health.

2. **Helps You Develop Stronger Relationships**

    When you feel connected to other people, you'll have better mental and physical health overall. Additionally, positive relationships with your peers make you less likely to engage in negative behaviors. Positive relationships also impact your personality and make your life more fun! It can help you develop a sense of self-awareness and empathy.
    It can help you to trust and rely on others more easily, making you less suspicious. While relationship development can help you feel more connected and loved, none of this can happen without you learning to channel your emotions positively.

3. **Fuel Your Productivity and Creativity**

    Whether you're happy, sad, angry, or just exhausted, your emotions fuel your productivity and creativity, and channeling emotions can enhance them.

    You may have often noticed that whenever you're feeling good about something, you feel motivated and excited and try to work even harder and be more productive. As a result, you end up getting so much more done in a short time. Creativity is also an important tool for problem-solving. It can help you see things from an absolutely unique perspective, develop new ideas, and find answers to tricky problems. However, stress or negative emotions can put a damper on how much you can get done and your creativity, so it is important to be vigilant about dealing with your emotions instead of keeping them stuffed inside.

4. **Communicate Better and Connect with Others**

    When you work on your social skills and grip your emotions, you open up effective communication lines and allow for a more honest connection with the person you're talking to. This can lead to a closer relationship, great communication, and a deeper understanding between you.

As a matter of fact, people are more likely to listen to you when emotions are involved in the communication pipeline. When people can hear and understand your feelings, they are more likely to respond in a way that benefits both of you. In other words, emotions are a very natural and full part of your communication network and must never be ignored. Once you start practicing channeling your emotions, it will reflect in your improved relationships with everyone around you.

Exercises to Channel Emotions Effectively

The best thing about channeling 'positive' emotions is that they make you feel good and bring several other benefits. According to some studies (Fredrickson, 2001), it is beneficial to experience more positive than negative emotions in a ratio of 3:1 (i.e., three times more positive emotions). So, below are some techniques and exercises to help you with that.

1. **Keeping Track of Your Emotions**
   In this exercise, you will have to label and record the positive emotions you experience daily. To start with, make a long list of all the positive emotions you're familiar with; this will help you recognize your emotions later on during the day as you experience them.
   So, at the end of each day, spend some time thinking about all the things you did, situations you were involved in, or the people you interacted with, and focus on how you felt in all of these scenarios. Your list will help you recognize or label the emotions at this stage. Ask yourself questions like, 'was I happy? Did I feel amused? Was I feeling proud?'
   This exercise helps you channel your emotions by seeing where the positive emotions you're already experiencing in your everyday life are.

You will become more and more aware of positive emotions and will recognize the situations, people, or activities that trigger them.

2. **Multiplying a Single Emotion**
   For this exercise, you will have to pick a positive emotion you want to improve. For instance, if you want to increase feelings of 'joy,' you may choose to use this exercise.
   Start by thinking about different situations you have experienced in your life, and you feel joyful. Make a list of as many such situations as possible. Initially, it is quite possible that you feel overwhelmed by this and come up with nothing! Don't panic; try focusing on simple things; perhaps there's a song that brings about feelings of joy. Or is there a dress you simply love and feel joy wearing? Perhaps there's a food or your favorite ice cream that makes you feel joyful often?
   The goal is to think about realistic situations that you can do at any time of the day. So, once you have the list ready, you can now use these trigger situations or activities to feel this emotion anytime you want. Try indulging in at least 3 of these activities daily to add more 'joy' to your life. Imagine that they are your daily dose of five emotion essentials!

3. **It's Time to Build a Treasure Chest!**
   Yes, we are building a treasure chest of gold! Oh no! It is not gold, but something even more precious, i.e., your positive emotions. Life has sneaky ways of pushing stress onto our shoulders, but we must stay vigilant to find our way back to positive feelings. To help you with this, you need a treasure box full of positive emotions. So, every time you need one, you can just go to the treasure box and get it.
   Building a 'treasure chest' of positive emotions is about collecting different positive memories and experiences from your life. It could be anything from photos with your friends or family, your favorite dress, a gift that you prize most, some souvenirs, an award that you won, inspirational quotes, your favorite childhood toy, cards, or love notes from

friends or family. In short, it's all about making a collection of all the reminders of things that are dear to you.

You can use a box or a small chest to get into this exercise's whole idea, but if you don't want anything fancy, it can be as simple as a binder or a file folder. You can also make a poster or photo collage or a pinboard collection. But whatever you do, it must be something you can touch. You also should be really selective about what goes inside your treasure collection. Obviously, you can rearrange, add, or take things out as you go.

Once you have the treasure box of positive emotions, you can turn to it every time you feel upset or gloomy. Spend some time going through the contents of this box or folder to relive the positive memories and fill yourself with positive emotions. You can also do this daily to add more positivity to your day instead of waiting for something negative to happen before diving into your "happy box.".

4. **Make It a Habit to Practice Gratitude**

   One simple way to open the gateway for more positive emotions is to practice gratitude on a daily basis. Appreciating all the positive things and experiences you're already experiencing in your life makes you more present and receptive toward more positivity. So, make it a habit to practice gratitude regularly before you go to bed by counting all the things that you're grateful for.

5. **Try Reframing Some Emotions**

   Sometimes you will experience overwhelming situations that bring up many negative feelings. One helpful strategy to deal with such difficult situations is to reframe or reappraise an event in a more positive light. So probe yourself with questions, like, 'what exactly do I feel? What are the things that made me feel like this? Could there be other emotional possibilities for this situation? Can I cope with this emotion in a better way? While it may be hard to do, there is always something positive in every situation, and by probing yourself with these questions, you will be actively reframing your experience and thoughts. This will eventually help you develop a more positive reaction to that event or similar situations.

6. **Pause and Figure out the What and Why**

    It sounds basic to think of "what & why" as a useful technique because we all know it, but do we really know it now? Usually, the' what and why' usually gets blurred in the heat of emotion, particularly strong negative emotion.

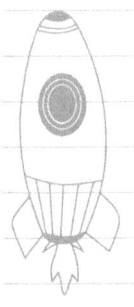

    So, it is highly recommended that you pause for a moment and think carefully about what you're really feeling at that moment. While you're trying to put a name to what you're experiencing, it will also help to understand all the things that made you feel this way. Your emotions don't exist in a void, so there's always one or more factors that lead to an emotion. This small check over your emotions will help you control and channel them better, and you'll soon become the master of your emotions.

7. **Escape the Trap of Overthinking**

    When it comes to channeling your emotions, the essential thing is learning to keep a balance. We already mentioned that suppressing your emotions is never the answer; however, this doesn't mean you end up dwelling on negative thoughts.

    The more you think about negative events or feelings, the greater the risk of falling into the trap of rumination is. So as soon as you notice that you're falling for the rumination trap, just steer your thoughts away from it gently.

So, Where Does That Leave You?

You must understand that learning to channel your emotions is a process; you only get better at it if you practice regularly. Another thing to remember is that the goal of channeling your emotions is not to suppress or deny the existence of negative emotions because even negative emotions have a purpose.

Your goal must be to regulate the feelings you're experiencing in a situation and steer them in a positive and more productive direction. After all, your tween years will not last forever, so better make the best of them while you can!

Conclusion

Being a tween is a very significant stage of self-development. At this age, you slowly start to become your own person. You begin constructing an identity with unique, interesting opinions, beliefs, and ideas. Being a pre-teen is a time in life when you begin having more meaningful relationships with your friends. If you take a moment to think about how different your interactions with your friends were just a few years ago, you'll notice that the time you spend and the conversations you have with them are much richer and more interesting.

While you must navigate many challenges as a tween, you can't deny that you have a growing and exciting sense of independence. This change can make you feel confident about your capabilities and encourage you to explore your interests and try new things. Spending less time with your parents and taking on different responsibilities can help you learn many things about what you can and can't do. This, however, doesn't mean that being a pre-teen is a sign that you should get distant from your parents. It simply means that you'll eventually figure out new ways to spend quality time with each other.

While being a tween is exciting in many ways, it can also be stressful and overwhelming at times. Being a pre-teen has its own difficulties, like more homework and chores. You may feel pressured by the academic and household-related expectations that you have to meet. Not to mention, you probably feel misunderstood and lost most of the time.

Fortunately, now that you have read this book, you know everything you need to know about navigating life as a tween. You are well-prepared to embark on your journey toward independence, make new friends, and deal with social anxiety. You also understand how to channel your emotions more effectively and how to be smart about using technology.

References

5 types of social skills deficit. (2016, October 29). Masters in Special Education Degree Program Guide |. https://www.masters-in-special-education.com/lists/5-types-of-social-skills-deficit/

Amy Morin, L. (2019, March 27). 7 social skills you should start teaching your child now. Verywell Family. https://www.verywellfamily.com/seven-social-skills-for-kids-4589865

Epperson, A. (2020, November 3). The importance of teaching social skills. PBIS Rewards. https://www.pbisrewards.com/blog/the-importance-of-teaching-social-skills/

Javed, A. (2021, April 15). Types of social skills with characteristics and Social skills list. EngloPedia. https://englopedia.com/social-skills-with-characteristics-and-types-with-detail/

Reynolds, N. (2020, October 12). 10 important social skills you need to teach your teen now. Raising Teens Today. https://raisingteenstoday.com/10-important-social-skills-you-need-to-teach-your-teen-now/

Understanding trouble with social skills. (2019, August 5). Understood. https://www.understood.org/en/articles/trouble-with-social-skills

Viktor Sander B. Sc., B. A., Natalie Watkins, M. S., & Morin, D. A. (2022, January 7). What are social skills? (definition, examples & importance). SocialSelf. https://socialself.com/blog/social-skills-definition/

What are social skills? & why are social skills important? (n.d.). Discovery Building Sets. https://discoverybuildingsets.com/blogs/dbs-articles/what-are-social-skills

What are Social Skills? Definition and Examples. (n.d.). Indeed Career Guide. https://www.indeed.com/career-advice/career-development/social-skills

Meleen, M., & More, R. (n.d.). What are tweens? LoveToKnow. https://teens.lovetoknow.com/What_are_Tweens

Middle school ages. (n.d.). Togetheragainstbullying.org. https://www.togetheragainstbullying.org/tab/targets/middle-school-ages/

O'Donnell, J. (2008, October 29). Defining the tween years for parents. Verywell Family. https://www.verywellfamily.com/what-is-a-tween-3288580

Sharon Martin, L. (2016, November 10). 26 questions to help kids know themselves better. Psych Central. https://psychcentral.com/blog/imperfect/2016/11/26-questions-to-help-kids-know-themselves-better

Bacsi, K. (2021, November 17). How to help a friend with social anxiety: 8 tips. The Recovery Village Drug and Alcohol Rehab. https://www.therecoveryvillage.com/mental-health/social-anxiety-disorder/how-to-help-a-friend-with-social-anxiety/

Can a person with social anxiety succeed in life? (n.d.). Quora. https://www.quora.com/Can-a-person-with-social-anxiety-succeed-in-life

Felman, A. (2020, September 7). Social anxiety disorder: Causes, symptoms, and treatment. Medicalnewstoday.com. https://www.medicalnewstoday.com/articles/176891

15 tips for building self-esteem and confidence in teens. (n.d.). Big Life Journal. https://biglifejournal.com/blogs/blog/build-self-esteem-confidence-teens

Cherry, K. (2021, May 26). 11 signs of low self-esteem. Verywell Mind. https://www.verywellmind.com/signs-of-low-self-esteem-5185978

Courtney E. Ackerman, M. A. (2018, May 23). What is Self-Esteem? A Psychologist Explains. Positivepsychology.com. https://positivepsychology.com/self-esteem/

Low self-esteem in adolescents: What are the root causes? (n.d.). Psychology Today. https://www.psychologytoday.com/us/blog/inside-out-outside-in/202206/low-self-esteem-in-adolescents-what-are-the-root-causes

Low Self-Esteem in Teens. (n.d.). Muhsd.org. https://echs.muhsd.org/echs/student-services/mental-health-library/low-self-esteem-in-teens

Clark, K. M. (2018, August 16). 10 easy ways anyone can help the new kid at school. Your Teen Magazine. https://yourteenmag.com/social-life/teenagers-friends/10-easy-ways-anyone-can-help-the-new-kid-at-school

Latumahina, D. (2010, July 15). 7 ways to use Humor to make new friends. Life Optimizer. https://www.lifeoptimizer.org/2010/07/15/how-to-make-new-friends/

Lusinski, N., & Moore, S. (2018, June 19). These 21 qualities are essential in any lifelong friend. Bustle. https://www.bustle.com/life/qualities-of-a-good-friend

Morris, A. (2018, August 17). 14 ways to find good friends no matter what your age. Lifehack. https://www.lifehack.org/794675/good-friends

Riter, S. (n.d.). 22 reasons why is it important to have A good friend. Theredheadriter.com. https://theredheadriter.com/2014/05/22-reasons-why-is-it-important-to-have-a-good-friend/

Tessina, T. (2019, February 25). 5 ways to charm the pants off everyone in the room. YourTango. https://www.yourtango.com/experts/dr-tina-tessina/turn-your-charm

van der Zande, I., Founder, K., & Executive Director. (2012, March 8). What if I get lost? Kidpower International; Kidpower Teenpower Fullpower International. https://www.kidpower.org/library/article/getting-lost/

What is the real definition of A true friend? (n.d.). Lifelot.Co.Nz. https://www.lifelot.co.nz/Blog/97/what-is-the-real-definition-of-a-true-friend

Wooll, M. (n.d.). What are the qualities of a good friend? 11 characteristics. Betterup.com https://www.betterup.com/blog/qualities-of-a-good-friend

Harrin, E. (2022, April 12). 5 tips for better decision making (with process). Rebel's Guide to Project Management; Rebel\'s Guide to Project Management. https://rebelsguidetopm.com/5-tips-for-making-better-decisions-every-day/

SHEROES - the women-only social network. (n.d.). Sheroes.com https://sheroes.com/articles/what-does-being-independent-really-mean/Mzc4Nw==

The importance of being independent. (2021, July 2). Del. Psych. Services. https://www.delawarepsychologicalservices.com/post/the-importance-of-being-independent

What being independent means to me - NCS Grad, Ellie. (n.d.). Wearencs.com https://wearencs.com/connect/what-being-independent-means-me-ncs-grad-ellie

Cyberbullying Research Center. (n.d.). Smart social networking: Fifteen tips for teens. Cyberbullying Research Center https://cyberbullying.org/smart-social-networking

Jill Christensen, C. N. P. (2021, May 28). Children and screen time: How much is too much? Mayo Clinic Health System. https://www.mayoclinichealthsystem.org/hometown-health/speaking-of-health/children-and-screen-time

Made in the USA
Middletown, DE
31 January 2023